FOUNDER **UN** FRIENDLY

CHARLIE O'DONNELL

FOUNDER UN FRIENDLY

WHAT INVESTORS WON'T TELL YOU ABOUT GETTING FUNDED

WILEY

Copyright © 2026 by John Wiley & Sons, Inc. All rights reserved, including rights for text and data mining and training of artificial intelligence technologies or similar technologies.

Published by John Wiley & Sons, Inc., Hoboken, New Jersey.

No part of this publication may be reproduced, stored in a retrieval system, or transmitted in any form or by any means, electronic, mechanical, photocopying, recording, scanning, or otherwise, except as permitted under Section 107 or 108 of the 1976 United States Copyright Act, without either the prior written permission of the Publisher, or authorization through payment of the appropriate per-copy fee to the Copyright Clearance Center, Inc., 222 Rosewood Drive, Danvers, MA 01923, (978) 750-8400, fax (978) 750-4470, or on the web at www.copyright.com. Requests to the Publisher for permission should be addressed to the Permissions Department, John Wiley & Sons, Inc., 111 River Street, Hoboken, NJ 07030, (201) 748-6011, fax (201) 748-6008, or online at http://www.wiley.com/go/permission.

The manufacturer's authorized representative according to the EU General Product Safety Regulation is Wiley-VCH GmbH, Boschstr. 12, 69469 Weinheim, Germany, e-mail: Product_Safety@wiley.com.

Trademarks: Wiley and the Wiley logo are trademarks or registered trademarks of John Wiley & Sons, Inc. and/or its affiliates in the United States and other countries and may not be used without written permission. All other trademarks are the property of their respective owners. John Wiley & Sons, Inc. is not associated with any product or vendor mentioned in this book.

Limit of Liability/Disclaimer of Warranty: While the publisher and the authors have used their best efforts in preparing this work, including a review of the content of the work, neither the publisher nor the authors make any representations or warranties with respect to the accuracy or completeness of the contents of this work and specifically disclaim all warranties, including without limitation any implied warranties of merchantability or fitness for a particular purpose. No warranty may be created or extended by sales representatives, written sales materials or promotional statements for this work. The fact that an organization, website, or product is referred to in this work as a citation and/or potential source of further information does not mean that the publisher and authors endorse the information or services the organization, website, or product may provide or recommendations it may make. This work is sold with the understanding that the publisher is not engaged in rendering professional services. The advice and strategies contained herein may not be suitable for your situation. You should consult with a specialist where appropriate. Further, readers should be aware that websites listed in this work may have changed or disappeared between when this work was written and when it is read. Neither the publisher nor authors shall be liable for any loss of profit or any other commercial damages, including but not limited to special, incidental, consequential, or other damages.

For general information on our other products and services or for technical support, please contact our Customer Care Department within the United States at (800) 762-2974, outside the United States at (317) 572-3993 or fax (317) 572-4002.

Wiley also publishes its books in a variety of electronic formats. Some content that appears in print may not be available in electronic formats. For more information about Wiley products, visit our web site at www.wiley.com.

Library of Congress Cataloging-in-Publication Data is Available:

ISBN 9781394369874 (Cloth)
ISBN 9781394369898 (ePub)
ISBN 9781394369881 (ePDF)

COVER DESIGN: PAUL MCCARTHY
COVER ART: © GETTY IMAGES | FOTOGRAZIA
AUTHOR PHOTO: COURTESY OF THE AUTHOR

SKY10148114_022726

To Mom and Dad, who I wish I could have shared this with.

*To Aja, the most honest, resilient,
and patient person I have ever met. I love you.*

To my daughter, Mirren. Daddy loves you.

Contents

Foreword by Ben McKean, Founder and CEO, Hungryroot   *ix*
Introduction   *xiii*

1. Free Your Mind: Dispelling Myths About Startups and Venture Capital   1
2. Show Me the Money: Who Gets Funded and Why?   29
3. I'm Putting Together a Team: Attracting Help and Support   49
4. You Can't Handle the Truth: Being Rigorous and Honest with Yourself   75
5. There's No Crying in Baseball: Doing the Hard Work   101
6. Keep Your Friends Close: The Importance of Trust   111
7. To Infinity . . . and Beyond! Going Big   119
8. Sell Me This Pen: Getting Ready to Raise   139
9. These Are Not the Droids You're Looking For: The Pitch   171
10. Dogs and Cats, Living Together: Mass Hysteria! Getting Yeses and Nos   211

Final Thoughts   227
Acknowledgments   231
About the Author   233
Index   235

Foreword

Ben McKean,
Founder and CEO, Hungryroot

In the startup ecosystem, silence is rarely an option. We live in an industry dominated by noise—by the relentless drumbeat of "crushing it," the curated serendipity of Twitter threads, and the polished narratives of overnight success. Founders are conditioned to project invincibility, and investors are conditioned to project omniscience. It is a dance of optimism that, while necessary to fuel innovation, often obscures the mechanical realities of how businesses are actually built and funded.

I have known Charlie O'Donnell for over a decade, and if there is one defining characteristic of his career, it is his refusal to participate in that performative dance. In a world of polite ambiguity, Charlie deals in the currency of absolute transparency and clarity.

We first met back in January 2011 through the Startup Leadership Program (SLP). At the time, I was navigating the early, turbulent waters of building a company, and the startup ecosystem was much smaller then. Everyone knew everyone, but you didn't really *know* someone until the chips were down.

My moment of clarity with Charlie came during a time of distinct instability. I was facing a situation where two of my board members had decided to step aside while our company struggled to survive.

In the venture world, that is a vulnerable moment. It creates a vacuum of uncertainty and signals potential risk to employees and outsiders. It is the exact moment when fair-weather connections usually go quiet, waiting to see if the ship steadies or sinks.

I knew who to reach out to: Charlie O'Donnell. He wasn't on my board, and he had no fiduciary obligation to hold my hand through the chaos. But he offered to help, to offer perspective, and simply to be around when things were getting tough. That moment has stayed with me for years because it perfectly encapsulates who Charlie is for founders: helpful, honest, and present, not just when the graph is up and to the right, but when the narrative gets messy.

That integrity is exactly why, when it came time to build Hungryroot, I knew who I wanted in my corner. That early interaction led me to reach out to Charlie, and he eventually led our first venture capital financing round.

However, *helpful* does not mean *nice* in the conventional, comforting sense. If you are lucky enough to have Charlie critique your startup pitch, you quickly learn that he pulls no punches. He doesn't do the "compliment sandwich." He doesn't nod along to a flawed business model to spare your feelings. He dissects the logic, challenges the assumptions, and tells you exactly why the idea won't work in its current form.

For years, that level of candid, structural feedback was limited to the founders who could get on his calendar or catch him at an event. With *Founder Unfriendly*, Charlie is finally sharing that version of himself with the rest of the world.

One of the core reasons Charlie and I have stayed connected over the years is a shared philosophy regarding what actually makes a company work. It's a concept he has written about extensively, and one that became the cornerstone of my journey with Hungryroot: falling in love with the problem, not the product.

This sounds simple, perhaps even cliché, until you are the one holding the product you spent years building, realizing it isn't going to scale the way you thought it would. That is the crucible of the founder. At Hungryroot, we have achieved tremendous success, generating nearly a billion dollars in annual revenue and employing over 1,000 employees. But the path to get here was not a straight line. We didn't get stuck on a single solution. If we had fallen in love with our initial product iterations, we likely would have stalled out. Instead, we remained obsessed with the customer need—the problem of eating healthy in a modern, busy world. We chased that need relentlessly, even when it meant breaking our own models and rebuilding.

Charlie was one of the few voices who consistently reinforced that mindset. He understands that the "product" is just a vehicle for solving the problem, and if the vehicle is broken, you get a new one. You don't abandon the journey.

This brings us to the heart of this book. *Founder Unfriendly* is a provocative title, but it is perhaps the most honest description of the venture capital landscape you will find. As Charlie outlines within these pages, raising capital isn't about charm, luck, or even having a brilliant product. It is about alignment.

Building Hungryroot has been the professional privilege of my life, but it has been incredibly hard. The press releases highlight the milestones, the revenue figures, and the growth metrics. They rarely capture the friction, the doubt, and the sheer grind required to align a business with the venture model.

Real wins require real work. They require an understanding of the machinery you are trying to plug into. When a VC tells you no, as Charlie explains, they aren't necessarily missing your potential. They are calculating whether your plan matches the size, speed, and shape of outcomes their fund model depends on.

Too many founders view fundraising as a game to be won, a puzzle where if you just say the right buzzwords, the check will clear. Charlie dismantles that myth. He shows you what the VC is actually solving for. He explains risk not as a vague concept, but as a mathematical and structural reality for the investor.

Reading this book is like sitting across from Charlie at a coffee shop in Brooklyn or facing him on one of those feedback panels. It might not always be what you *want* to hear. He isn't going to tell you that your passion alone is enough. He isn't going to validate a business model that doesn't fit the asset class just to be polite.

But it is exactly what you *need* to hear.

In a world full of "founder-friendly" platitudes that ultimately lead to misaligned cap tables and painful board meetings, Charlie offers something far more valuable: the truth. He provides the context you need to stop gaming the system and start understanding the business you are actually building.

If you are ready to move past the clichés of "thinking big" and get down to the practical realities of funding and building a massive company, you are holding the right guide.

Introduction

Here's what you'll get from this book: clarity on whether to raise outside investment, a sharper story than when you started, an honest read on your chances, and a practical system for building investor trust.

I've put this upfront because it was the first piece of feedback my wife ever gave me after reading it—that the benefits weren't clear and they didn't come early enough. You have Aja to thank for this opening sentence.

Before I even wrote this book, I had a conversation with my editor about the title. We settled on "Founder Unfriendly" right off the bat, given my charming personality, but the subtitle proved a bit more difficult.

ChatGPT says that a good subtitle is supposed to do the following:

1. Clarify the book's topic or audience.

2. Add specificity or promise a benefit.

3. Include keywords or hooks for search/discovery.

So, who is this book for? Is it just for people seeking venture capital funding, or can it be for anyone needing an investor of any kind? I'm writing this book for anyone seeking funding for anything—from a technology founder pitching Midas List venture capitalists (VCs) to a corporate exec trying to get more budget for a new initiative.

That also includes foodies trying to get a fresh pasta place up and running, or someone building a play space for working parents to take their kids to. My hope is that while I'm a career VC who mostly worked with tech startups, the lessons about gaining someone else's trust to secure their capital will still be relevant to all sorts of people seeking to get backed.

Part of the reason why I wanted to extend the audience is because who you should pitch for an idea isn't always clear. Some VCs write small checks, and some high-net-worth individuals write very large ones. Figuring out stage isn't so cut and dry either—as some angels might not want to hear from you until you have revenue, while there are some venture capital funds that often fund two people and a pitch deck.

Even messier is what kinds of companies get funded by investors. Blank Street Coffee secured $20 million in funding from venture capitalists in 2023, while your average local coffee shop might borrow money from friends and family just to get one location up and running.

The same VC firm that backed Blank, General Catalyst, also backed one of the largest AI models in use today.

That's why this book will also cover the basics of who should even take venture capital money and what you're signing up for when you do. It's meant to be relevant to anyone who says, "I think I have a great idea, but I don't have the money to get it off the ground."

I'll also share some thoughts about the ways this game appears rigged.

I once found myself in a long email exchange with a female founder who challenged the venture ecosystem over how women are treated. She cited the familiar stats—2% of funding going to women, systemic exclusion, male-dominated panels.

I didn't disagree with the macro problems around the tech industry's treatment and support of women.

In fact, I've backed women at more than double the industry rate and Black founders at eight times the average. I personally invited her to curated events I host specifically to create access.

But none of that landed.

She was asking for acknowledgment. And that's where I often fail.

Because my instinct—the operator, the competitor in me—is to skip acknowledgment and go straight to tactics:

> *"Yes, bias exists. Now here's how to run circles around the guy they're also considering funding."*

I don't linger on unfairness because unfairness can't be fixed during the pitch. No founder has ever beaten bias by winning the moral argument. They beat it by outplaying everyone else in the pipeline: clearer pitch, louder ask, stronger proof, shameless follow-up.

But to her, my urgency to get tactical sounded like dismissal. She heard:

> *"Stop complaining."*

What I meant was:

> *"Stop getting out-executed."*

Here's what I learned in that exchange:

Telling someone "Here's how to win anyway" will be heard as "Your pain doesn't matter" if you don't first say "I see it."

Track records don't absolve you from the responsibility to empathize. You can back dozens of women and underrepresented founders and still be experienced as "part of the system."

Some founders want the system explained. Others want the system condemned. If you confuse the two, you'll waste oxygen and lose both.

I don't believe you can argue bias out of an investor. I believe you can put a better deal in front of them. That doesn't invalidate the emotional exhaustion of founders who are tired of being underestimated.

It's just the only lever I know that moves dollars.

I'm still working on remembering that before I hand someone the lever, I may need to say:

"You're right. It is unfair. Now—do you want to win anyway?"

Unfair doesn't mean unwinnable. I've spent 20 years watching founders crack the code, and the rest of this book is about how you can too.

What I won't be selling you is a quick and easy five-step process for anyone to follow and raise venture capital. Yes, there are better and worse ways to approach fundraising, and we'll talk about tactics, but fundraising isn't like chess, where there's a statistically "correct" move that definitively increases your chances of winning.

It's closer to improv theater—you can prep, but you also need to respond to what's in the room. That's hard to do if you don't understand what's going on in the room, and that's where this book comes in.

In James Carse's *Finite and Infinite Games*, he describes *finite* games as being played to win. The rules, players, and outcomes are known in advance. Surprise is treated as something to minimize, because too much of it could destabilize the contest. Players train, plan, and anticipate to control as much of the uncertainty as possible.

This is how I feel when I watch *Shark Tank*.

It's all very contained—you come on, pitch, and they either fund you or they don't. Nothing outside of those two outcomes happens. Contestants don't decide to stop working on their companies or pivot their model—and the sharks don't get so into the idea that they decide to join as employees. You also never hear of a founder impressing investors so much that after their company fails, they get hired to join another portfolio company of the investor.

All these outcomes are possible, but only when you think of fundraising more like an *infinite* game. This endeavor to raise is just a step along your continuing journey. You don't "win" an infinite game. The rules can evolve, new players can enter, and outcomes are open-ended. Here, surprise is not an interruption but the very point—because novelty, unexpected shifts, and reconfigurations are what keep the game alive.

In practice, this means you'll leave investor meetings stronger whether you walk out with a check.

You can't lose when you stop thinking of the goal as "raise a million dollars" and instead frame it as learning more about the nature of the problem you're trying to solve. When playing successfully means using feedback to make your business idea better, testing your story, and building lasting trust with influential people, the game becomes a better experience for more players.

After all, the investors you pitch are playing an infinite game—leveraging decades-long connections, building their network of multi-time founders, creating lasting reputations. That's probably how they got so successful in the first place. No VC expects anyone meeting or company to define their career. They're optimizing across portfolios, relationships, and years. Their meeting with you is an opportunity to learn and possibly the first step in a long-term trust-building exercise on their side.

I won't promise that you'll raise, but I can promise you that you'll feel better positioned on your journey be it with this idea, the next one, or just in the direction of your whole career. You'll stop feeling like you're stumbling through a rigged game and start feeling like you know how to play it on your own terms.

The perspective I'll bring to the table is one of a venture capitalist who has funded more than 100 companies, some to exits of hundreds of millions of dollars. Others are doing multiples of that in annual revenue. I worked for two of the most prominent firms in the industry: Union Square Ventures and First Round Capital, and then started my own firm, Brooklyn Bridge Ventures, where I raised three venture capital funds

I've also started small, local efforts, like a kayaking boathouse on the East River with an annual budget less than what I spent on my triathlon bike. I've also looked at the decks and financials of many small businesses—restaurants and alcohol brands—to help neighbors and friends.

Not everything needs to be VC backed and go public to be seen as a great success by those involved.

My hope is that you have a clearer idea of your chances and that you go through a more honest conversation with yourself and others as to whether *this* is the idea you want to dedicate all your time to.

What you can expect is some clarity on where the bar is for fundraising success and some dispelled notions about how investment works. I'll also try to push you to make sure the idea you're working on is as vetted as it can be—that it's worth your time to be working on it and asking others for money.

We'll talk about what's in your control, what's not, and how trust works in the investment process. And yes, we'll talk pitch decks and getting meetings and all that stuff—after we've established that you've got the right idea to pitch and that this is the right kind of money to be looking for.

You should feel encouraged and motivated after reading this, but I want to be clear about what I'm trying to get out of you.

I don't just want you to feel good about your idea. I want you to test it, pressure it, and strengthen it. Encouragement without action is just a pep talk. My goal is to give you the push to do the uncomfortable work that makes your company fundable.

I want you to believe you belong in the game, but this book isn't about handing you an easy win. It's about equipping you to approach fundraising as a tough, ongoing practice that will ultimately make your company better. If you walk away with both confidence and momentum, then I've done my job.

As for keywords, since you're reading this, I'll assume whatever title we settled on worked to get you here.

FOUNDER UN FRIENDLY

Chapter 1

Free Your Mind

Dispelling Myths About Startups and Venture Capital

Some people ease into starting up their own business by bootstrapping. Nights. Weekends. No outside pressure. No headlines.

Side hustles and lifestyle businesses are the cat ownership of the startup world. It takes real work—shots, toys, the carrier—but the cat doesn't care when you leave for your day job.

A simple piece of software in a niche area can be worked on when you have free time. You can answer customer emails when you get home from work. This approach will proliferate as artificial intelligence (AI) gets better.

Finding a co-founder, raising investor money, and hiring for growth now all goes beyond fluffy pet ownership. It's like having an actual child.

The most important and fulfilling job I've ever had in my life is being a parent. There is nothing better than having a three-year-old spread her arms out wide and say, "I love you this much" or jump in a pool for the first time without someone catching her and say, "I did it!"

There's also nothing more difficult than that same three-year-old thrashing wildly on the floor covered in tears because she doesn't want to go to bed, or even worse, because you gave her a piece of toilet paper to blow her nose instead of the tissue that she asked for.

Being a startup founder often feels the same way. Everybody tells you it's the most meaningful thing you'll ever do—until you're in it, exhausted, overwhelmed, and wondering if you've made a terrible mistake.

In a recent conversation with Na'ama Moran, a founder friend and a parent, we both admitted what few founders will say out loud: you can love the thing you created and still hate what it's doing to you. You can be proud and burned out at the same time.

You can win on paper and feel like you're losing your mind.

Na'ama co-founded Cheetah, a VC-backed wholesale restaurant supply business, and scaled it into a $150 million multistate operation. On paper, she did everything right. But after years of pushing through, she stepped down. Not because the company failed—but because she was burned out, emotionally wrecked, and questioning the entire system she had been operating inside.

The startup mythology doesn't leave room for that. It tells you this is what greatness feels like: stretched thin, emotionally fried, sleep-deprived, but still smiling for TechCrunch. Founders don't get to say "this sucks" without sounding ungrateful or weak.

But let's be real—sometimes it does suck. Pretending otherwise isn't strength.

It's denial.

One of the reasons why I think it sucks is because it doesn't get you the main benefit you were looking for when you started—agency. People start companies to be their own boss. They want control. Impact. A seat at the table.

Yet, when you're out begging investors for capital, have no full-time employees, and have a product struggling to get users, you don't feel like you're in the driver's seat.

I think Bane described it best in the *Dark Knight Rises*:

"Do you *feel* in charge?"

I'm not saying you shouldn't start a company—but we should all be honest about what you're signing up for when you do, particularly when you seek investor capital to fund it. What you're doing is adding risk. You're on an otherwise predictable career path and taking a sharp detour. It could be a shortcut to wealth, fame, and influence, but it could also be a dead end that requires you to double back. You might have to start all over to rebuild the savings you burned and to restart the steady, upward career trajectory you traded in for a chance at something much bigger.

Years ago, I led an investment into a local ice cream shop called Ample Hills. It was started by a Brooklyn couple, Brian and Jackie—people who seemed to be put on this earth to create the kind of joy that one uniquely experiences in an ice cream shop.

It had become a Cinderella story, selling out of all their ice cream just days after opening. Bob Iger himself, CEO of Disney, was one of the shop's biggest fans. They wound up opening a big factory and a shop right on the boardwalk in Disney World.

I could write a book about what happened over the next six years—someone should—but the short story is that the company ran into some cash flow issues caused by cost overruns, delayed shop openings, and some incredibly difficult investors. They were forced into bankruptcy—losing the business entirely while being saddled with a ton of personal debt.

They had two kids, a mortgage, and no easy path back into the workforce.

As one of their venture capital investors, I always knew this was a possibility—but I've always regretted not making sure they sat with that idea.

We never had a serious conversation about it.

I should have had them acknowledge it—to say it to me—that the chance of taking this national is more important than avoiding failure.

3

Free Your Mind

That's how you must think when you take outside capital—that having a shot at making it big is so important that you're okay with also increasing the chance at losing at all. Any founder who takes outside capital should sit with the idea of what would happen if they did go out of business. They should picture it—what would you do the morning after, when you wake up and you don't have your business to run. You have no income—you've taken money from some of your closest relationships and lost it. You've announced to the world that your business has gone under.

How would you feel?

What would you do?

If that sounds like the worst day of your life, good. Picture it. Sit with it.

If you still want to do this . . . now you're ready.

Should I Raise or Should I Go?

A surprising number of founders start with the assumption that raising money is the first step. They'll say, "I can't build this without capital," as if VC is the default price of admission. Raising venture capital isn't just a financial choice—it's an agreement to operate inside a very specific system: speed, scrutiny, dilution, expectations, a binary outcome curve, and a company trajectory that often looks nothing like the calm, profitable business many people actually want to run.

Needing money *cannot* be the only reason to raise. Saving the company is not the same thing as scaling it. Venture capital is not life support. If anything, it's an accelerant—and accelerants only work when there's already something burning.

This section exists to help you pause and ask a more fundamental question:

Does your business—and do *you*—actually fit what the venture system demands?

If not, that's not a failure. It's clarity.

Plenty of great companies are not venture-backed companies.

Here's a checklist founders should walk through *before* deciding on taking outside equity investment:

1. **The market supports a billion-dollar outcome.**

   Most exits won't be that large, but acquirers rarely pay a few hundred million dollars unless they believe they can *triple the size of the business* once they own it. If the ceiling is lower than that, the venture model becomes misaligned quickly.

2. **Winning the market actually matters.**

   Some markets reward being "one of many." Venture-backed markets usually don't. You don't want to be *a* coffee chain—you want to be *the* coffee chain. Value tends to concentrate in the top one or two players.

3. **Now is the right time to start this specific business.**

   Founders often raise because they're afraid someone else will. The better question is whether *this is the right moment*: a regulatory shift, technological inflection, or behavioral change that creates an opening.

4. **There's a believable path to compounding growth.**

   Venture capital is gas on a fire. It doesn't create the flame. Compounding growth means that each new customer makes the next one easier to acquire—growth accelerates because the business itself reinforces it. If growth remains linear, adding capital won't change the trajectory.

5. **Unit economics improve with scale.**

   In venture-scale businesses, the one thousandth customer should be cheaper and more profitable to serve than the tenth. If costs rise faster than revenue, or margins collapse as you grow, the model doesn't bend toward venture outcomes.

6. **Customer acquisition can be repeated by a team, not just the founder.**

   Founder hustle can get the first few customers. But venture-backed companies need acquisition methods that can be taught, repeated, and improved with budget. If growth depends entirely on founder charisma or personal relationships, it won't scale.

7. **Raising capital unlocks something meaningful—not just survival.**

   If the only pitch is "we're out of money," that's not a venture case. Funding should accelerate progress that's already happening, not act as a temporary life raft for something that isn't working.

8. **The business becomes stronger as it gets bigger.**

   Network effects, switching costs, accumulated data, brand—something should make the next customer *easier* to win. Venture scale requires momentum that compounds as the company grows.

9. **There is a real moat, or at least a plausible path to one.**

   A moat is anything that makes the business hard to copy: proprietary data, a unique distribution advantage, switching costs, genuine technology, or a reinforcing network effect. Venture-backed companies need meaningful defensibility eventually, even if not immediately.

10. **Competition will intensify as you succeed—and speed matters.**

    If you prove there's real value in a market, larger or better-capitalized players will enter. Venture capital makes sense when *moving faster than competitors* is part of how you win.

11. You actually want to run a big, fast-moving company.

This seems obvious, but it isn't. The venture path means rapid hiring, more people to manage, bigger budgets, and less calm. Many founders want a profitable, steady business—and that is absolutely valid, but it's not the venture path.

12. You're ready for the scrutiny that comes with investor money.

Boards, reporting, metrics, questions, expectations. You can't take venture capital and then be surprised when people expect visibility and accountability. It's part of the deal.

13. You're comfortable with dilution.

Every dollar raised trades ownership for the possibility of a much larger outcome later. Some founders struggle with this emotionally. Venture only works if you're okay owning a smaller slice of a much bigger pie.

14. The upside is limited unless you raise capital.

Some companies can scale by reinvesting profits. Others hit a ceiling—they need capital to hire, build, or enter the market before the opportunity closes. Venture fits when outside money is required to capture the real upside.

15. You're okay with the binary nature of venture outcomes.

Venture is not designed for modest wins. It's designed for companies that either become very large or don't work at all. Founders need to be comfortable taking that kind of swing.

If you check most of these boxes, the venture model is likely aligned with your ambitions and your business.

If you don't, the takeaway is not "your idea isn't good."

It's "your idea might belong to a different, and often better, funding path."

This is the myth worth dispelling early:

Venture capital is not the default path for ambitious founders.

It's a specialized tool for a specific kind of company—and a specific kind of founder.

Famously Irrelevant

Whenever you read the advice of successful founders on how they raised or grew their companies, you must keep in mind the context about how they started.

Back in 2009, a founder swiped my credit card for a $2 charge while we sat on a park bench in Manhattan's West Village—using his phone. That might seem uneventful, and a little random, but back then you couldn't do that without an expensive credit card reader plugged into a wall. Those $2 were #477 and #478 to pass through the very first prototype of the Square—a tiny mobile credit card reader that plugged into the audio jack of a cell phone. You might think that's not much traction for a startup, but the company soon raised millions of dollars at a high valuation, including from the firm I worked for at the time, First Round Capital.

It helped that it was Jack Dorsey, the co-founder of Twitter, sitting next to me on that bench.

Someone could distill the moves he made into a "fundraising tips" post, but how much of it would be relevant to you if you didn't previously start a company that went public?

Plus, Jack never raised capital for Twitter, per se. Twitter was a pivot from a podcasting platform called Odeo that was founded by Ev Williams after he sold Blogger to Google. Jack was a contract engineer who had the idea for Twitter while working at Odeo but never raised the first round for it.

Most of the time you hear fundraising advice from exited founders, a lot of it won't apply to you directly. For one, those people raised their first funding years ago—before the current level of competition existed. It was easier to pitch LinkedIn, for example, when professional networking online didn't exist at all. Today's version of that, pitching LinkedIn for GenZ, is much more difficult because LinkedIn already exists—not to mention that technology has changed a ton since then.

My former boss Josh Kopelman, founder of First Round Capital, used to say that people always thought of him as the e-commerce expert having founded Half.com and sold it to eBay for $350 million. Yet, by his own admission, he founded the company before anyone had ever bought anything from their phones and before Facebook ads ever existed. The e-commerce landscape is so different today that he admits today's founders teach him more about e-commerce than he had ever learned.

If you can't just use the templates and tips of famously successful founders, how are you supposed to know how to do it?

Choose Your Character

There's a saying that history doesn't repeat itself, it rhymes.

That's true in fundraising too. You can't just lift someone else's game plan directly, but there are themes and personas that you can latch onto, or avoid. They each come with their upsides and downsides.

By no means is this an exhaustive list of personas of people who try raise but see if you find yourself in one or more of these.

Green Light

These are people who tend to raise money easily.

The Hacker-Pivoter

This is the fast builder—the one who can spin up products overnight, experiment with the newest tech, and quickly abandon what doesn't work. The most fundable version of this founder isn't just a great coder—they're already plugged into the community. They show up at events, comment on VC posts, and are known for their skills. That visibility makes it easy to get a first meeting.

Sometimes, these founders don't need a massive hit to validate themselves. Selling a small but meaningful product to a larger company can be enough to prove they can ship, execute, and deliver value. Kareem Amin, before founding Clay, started a company called Frame that was acquired by Sailthru in 2012. It wasn't a blockbuster exit, but it demonstrated that he could build something real that a venture-backed acquirer wanted. That kind of outcome establishes credibility and makes investors more willing to bet on whatever you decide to build next. For hacker-pivoters, reputation and proof points often matter more than any one idea.

The Industry Insider

Other founders come straight out of the industries they're serving. They know the customers, the lingo, and the influential people who can write checks. A real estate founder might raise from a network of real estate families. A recruiter might get money from top search executives in their space.

The big question here is, "How much of an insider are you?" Did you just work at Macys on the floor or did you own all merchandizing for menswear?

The upside is obvious: raising that first million or two can be relatively straightforward, and VCs love seeing customers double as investors—it's a built-in validation that the product matters. The risk is that these investors aren't always savvy about venture terms. Deals can end up with inflated valuations or messy cap tables. Arch, a platform for family offices, was backed by family offices themselves—a neat flywheel for customer adoption, but those deals aren't always aligned with broader venture norms. That can create friction when you eventually need institutional capital. Industry insiders can raise quickly, but they need to be careful about how those early deals set the stage for later rounds.

The Junior Staffer

Think startup employees from breakout companies or junior VC staffers. They don't have blank-check credibility, but they've seen the process up close. They know what a good deck looks like, what terms are standard, and which investors to approach. Their networks—former founders, bosses, and peers—often provide warm introductions.

These founders usually put together respectable pitches and avoid rookie mistakes. They can raise small rounds quickly, often with support from their former employers. But there's a risk: if their early career was all "rocket ship" growth, they may underestimate how brutal the grind can be.

It's like Derek Jeter winning four championships in his first five years—it sets up the belief that success is automatic. When the next idea isn't a rocket ship, reality hits harder. For junior staffers, fundraising skill comes naturally, but staying power must be earned.

Yellow Light

Fundraising success for these founders is a mixed bag.

The Executive

Some founders come straight out of senior roles in big companies. They carry impressive titles, deep networks, and years of management experience. On paper, that makes them look fundable—and often, they are. Investors figure their connections will open doors and their polish will make the company look credible.

But there's a catch. Many of these executives are motivated less by a burning problem and more by the idea of breaking out of the corporate grind. And most of them have never actually seen products get built well. Fortune 1,000 companies don't ship at startup speed or startup quality, and executives rarely get close to the trenches. That lack of scrappiness shows up quickly when they're expected to operate without layers of support, and it can leave them unprepared for the realities of building from zero.

The Credentialed Academic

Some founders come out of labs or research institutions with deep technical credibility. They bring patents, intellectual property, or expertise in fields like biotech, materials, or AI. But academic pedigree alone isn't enough. The DNA of the team has to include startup experience—either by pairing the academic with a business co-founder or by spinning out of an institution that already has a track record of launching companies.

The strongest examples are when the academic isn't just a technologist hunting for someone else to commercialize their work, but when they've built their own industry ties—consulting, collaborating with companies, or otherwise staying close to the market. That combination of technical depth and market connectivity makes them fundable. Without it, investors worry they'll get stuck at the lab bench.

The Missionary Founder

Some founders are driven by a personal mission. They've lived the problem themselves or seen it up close—parents of a child with a medical condition, educators fed up with broken systems, immigrants navigating costly remittances. That authenticity makes them compelling storytellers and often draws in early believers.

When the mission overlaps with a lucrative market, this works beautifully. Investors love backing founders who clearly care and who bring real insight into customer pain. But it becomes a problem when the passion doesn't translate into profit. Missionary founders can struggle to understand why VCs care about margins and scale, and why "saving the world" isn't enough on its own. Without a path to making money, the mission alone won't sustain a venture-backed business.

The Celebrity or Influencer Founder

Some startups are built around the reach of a celebrity or influencer. The pitch is simple: millions of fans translate into millions of potential customers. That story can get investors interested, but the reality is riskier. Most of the time, the startup is just another side project. Celebrities often spread their attention across multiple ventures, and their teams lean on outsourced development shops that balloon in cost. Like an entourage, they attract people who see it more as a fame-and-money play than a disciplined company.

There are exceptions. Kim Kardashian was deeply involved in the creation of *Kim Kardashian: Hollywood*, the mobile role-playing game developed by Glu Mobile. She approved every outfit used in the game, participated in discussions around features and in-game events, and reviewed milestones from early alpha builds through to the final gold master. That level of attention made her involvement a genuine asset. But that's the rare case. For most celebrity-led startups, unless the star commits their time and influence at full strength, the company never escapes being just a vanity project.

Red Light

These founders will struggle to raise.

The Wealthy Hobbyist

Every so often you meet a founder who doesn't need outside money. They might come from family wealth, a lucrative professional career, or other sources outside the startup world. They can fund the early stages themselves, which on the surface seems like an advantage. But VCs usually keep their distance.

The problem isn't the money—it's the mindset. Wealthy hobbyists often feel like they don't need to be told anything, and they're not eager to grind through the hard parts of building. Without urgency or coachability, they struggle to build momentum. From the outside, it can look less like a company in the making and more like a side project with unlimited runway.

The Outsider

This is the founder who shows up with a product but no community presence, no warm intros, and no sense of how fundraising works. They're the type you might see pitching on *Shark Tank*—earnest, heads-down, but disconnected from the networks where capital flows.

The truth is that outsider status today is often self-inflicted. VCs aren't hiding. They publish thought leadership, show up at conferences, sit on panels, and post constantly on social media. In a world where there are free events every week with investors on stage, staying invisible is a choice. If you've been too inwardly focused on your business to engage at all, it's going to be almost impossible to get funded.

On top of that, outsiders often get the basics of fundraising wrong. They'll say their seed round should take them to a $2 million Series A—when in today's market that would be the world's tiniest A round. These kinds of mismatched expectations flag inexperience immediately and make VCs check out.

The Beggar

Another red flag is the founder who acts like a supplicant instead of a peer. They're so overwhelmed and intimidated by successful people that they can't bring themselves to make real asks. Instead, they hover on the sidelines, hoping someone with money or influence will notice them and offer help on their own time.

This posture undermines credibility immediately. Investors want to back leaders who see themselves as equals in the room, not petitioners waiting to be chosen. A founder who can't own their ask comes across as someone who doesn't truly believe they belong—and if they don't believe it, no one else will either.

Fundraising isn't about copying Jack Dorsey, or Kim Kardashian, or anyone else. It's about knowing the hand you're holding—the starting point you bring into the room—and playing it with clarity. Investors respond differently depending on whether you're a hacker, an insider, an academic, or a hobbyist.

That doesn't mean you're stuck in one lane forever. Hacker-pivoters can become insiders, missionaries can learn the business side, outsiders can choose to engage. But pretending you're something you're not only leads to frustration. The key is to recognize where you're starting, be honest about the advantages and disadvantages that come with it and raise money on terms that fit your persona—not someone else's mythology.

Winning Mindsets

Who you are matters, but your mindset counts just as much. You could have the best background on paper, but your approach, confidence, and character are the fuel in the engine.

Starting any kind of project—be it a company, a charity, or even a community garden—will be a series of ups and downs. Not everything will go your way. Every time you make some progress with one thing, something else goes off the rails.

Welcome to startup life.

In my experience, there are two categories of mindsets people have when setting out to raise for the first time. You can divide them up by combinations of the advantages they start out with and their mental and emotional approach.

Some of these "startup life" circumstances are beyond your control. There's nothing "anyone" can do about them. Others are solvable problems.

The thing about solvable problems is that not everyone has equal resources to solve them. This is a completely unfair fact of life. If you were born into money, for example, you can probably put more things into the "Things I can change or solve" group than someone who never had any money. If you come from a well-connected family with a big network, you undoubtedly have more ability to solve problems than someone who isn't connected to anyone or whose family just arrived in this country.

Let's call these two general categories of people "resourced" and "underresourced," which obviously gives you a different mindset going in. It can be a great help to know that you've got a big network and proximity to successful people.

Your assumptions around the influence you have on your own life matters as well. That's another category. Lots of people start with nothing and make it big. Some people also start with a lot and never really level up or make something of all the advantages they started out with. In my experience, people tend to either feel responsible for everything that happens to them, looking inward all the time for answers (or blame), or they feel like their life is mostly influenced by forces on the outside—by other people or systems.

We'll call the people who feel like most things are in their control "drivers" and the people who feel like the world is just taking them for a ride "passengers."

When you combine all the possibilities of which of the two groupings you're in, you wind up with the four mindsets in Figures 1.1 and 1.2.

Type	Belief & Locus	Attributes	Pros/Cons
The Inside Track	Driver—internal locus "I shape my outcomes."	Confident, well-networked, often white/male; seen as "default fundable." Pitch big visions, assume success, and leverage strong support systems.	Pro: Clear, bold pitch; knows how to "work the game." Con: May be untested, entitled, or skip hard work.
The Drifters	Passenger—external locus "Things happen to me."	Credentialed and steady but risk-averse. Favor safe ideas and blame setbacks on external forces.	Pro: Appear fundable on paper. Con: Lack urgency or breakout thinking; hard to get excited about.

Figure 1.1 Resourced Mindsets (Those with Financial Security, Network, Education)

Type	Belief & Locus	Attributes	Pros/Cons
The Fighters	Driver—internal locus "I shape my outcomes."	Scrappy and determined, they grind for every inch. Often overlooked at first, but impress with persistence and clarity of purpose.	Pro: Hustle, grit, self-awareness, purpose. Con: Lack networks, confidence, and momentum.
The Stranded	Passenger—external locus "Things happen to me."	Idealistic but disconnected. Often doubt themselves, don't ask for enough, and feel "lucky to be in the room." Wait for someone to discover them rather than driving their own story.	Pro: Sincere and thoughtful. Con: Lack networks, confidence, and momentum.

Figure 1.2 Underresourced Mindsets (Those Facing Financial, Systemic, or Network Barriers)

What you hear about fundraising depends a lot on whether you're talking to Resourced Drivers (Inside Track), Underresourced Drivers (Fighters), Resourced Passengers (Drifters), or Underresourced Passengers (The Stranded).

Resourced Drivers

Many of the most successful founders—the ones we are told we should look up to—have two things going for them. First, they're in the mindset of being a driver. That's pretty obvious. They act as if they can affect the world around them more than the world affects them. If they encounter a problem, they feel like they can do something about it.

Sometimes, you'll see this referred to as the "entrepreneurial mindset."

It's hard to separate having this kind of mindset from the fact that they're also likely to be well-resourced at the start. While they might not feel "privileged," they may have had a certain level of financial stability, housing stability and educational support that not everyone gets.

This doesn't necessarily mean "rich."

We tend to forget how difficult it can be for some people in "wealthy" countries and cities given how unevenly wealth can be distributed. Even in the United States, if you had stable housing, two parents with stable incomes, family stability, and a good education, you grew up in a fairly well-resourced environment compared to the average.

And, statistically, you are more likely to be white if you have all of those things.

I wish more entrepreneurial influencers acknowledged this. You often hear successful people say, "My family wasn't rich. My parents owned a small local business and they hustled. I learned that hustle from them and grew my fortune all on my own through hard work!"

What you're not hearing them say, even though they should, is, "I was really fortunate. I never had to choose between working on my business and having a roof over my head. My parents didn't need me to make money for them. I was able to bootstrap because they had the space for me to live at home and I wasn't obligated to pay my share of the food that I ate, or for rent or utilities."

That kind of thing makes all the hustling a little easier.

Combine that advantage with the feeling like they're driving and able to impact the world—and now they're basically Avengers. Having the means "and" the motivation can feel like a cloak of invincibility in a video game.

This, of course, assumes that they're comfortable with some level of risk. Not everyone is. Some people who grow up in successful environments don't want to do anything to mess that up. There's a lot of fear of failure for people who have never experienced it.

Resourced drivers might face a lot of pressure not to squander the opportunity to do something more traditionally successful, like becoming a well-respected doctor or lawyer. I might argue that these people aren't really drivers. They don't feel like they actually have the power to choose for themselves what they want to do. These folks are pushed into the passenger seat by their risk aversion—excelling in an otherwise "safe" field.

When they are willing to take a risk, resourced drivers tend to feel like their ideas are a train leaving the station—that they're pitching something that investors are lucky to get an opportunity to see. The results in an incredibly confident pitch that investors will feel compelled to lean into. When these folks talk about fundraising in podcasts or other interviews, you might feel like they're just cut from a different cloth than you—and that you'll never have that level of confidence no matter how convinced you are about an idea.

One place where initial confidence makes a huge difference is that the best fundraisers are also using their networks to leave no stone unturned in their own due diligence process for an idea. Their belief in an idea compounds because they were confident enough to put themselves out there to some incredibly successful and important people. When they build software for banks, they don't just ask a bank teller how they use software—they network their way to the CEO to get feedback.

When you get bank CEOs getting excited about your idea—selling investors on it is going to be a piece of cake.

On the other hand, being well-resourced sometimes leaves founders a bit lazy. They skip the grunt work of testing their assumptions by putting their idea up to discerning customers. While they have no problem sharing a vision with investors, but direct questions about competition or go to market are met with dismissal. They haven't quite done all the homework needed to properly vet their idea or hammer out a plan, nor have they considered the possibility that they're not right.

Some of these founders are going to be able to raise a first round of capital based on the strength of their networks and their unbridled confidence. Not to worry. They're very quickly going to have to learn some hard lessons. They might need to pivot or go through some really difficult periods in their startup when things aren't working (to their surprise). Some will recover—and it will all be a tremendous lesson for them. They'll learn not to make those bad assumptions ahead of time and learn a hard lesson on the amount of work it will take to succeed. While things might be easy for them upfront, it's not going to be smooth sailing for them all the way.

When they fail, they'll be back at it again with another idea—because they don't fear the scrutiny of failing and its impact on their trajectory.

These folks will make you feel like fundraising is a bit of an insider's club—because you can't figure out how they raised in the first place. They didn't have more traction than you did and it feels like their story is a bit of smoke and mirrors. Yet, both things can be true—that they did sell a big vision and vaporware to start, thanks to a big leg up, but they made that work and have turned it into something real.

You'll feel like you could have done the same with their kind of start, but you won't appreciate how much they've learned along the way and how good they've gotten as founders.

When you hear about fundraising from them, the way they say to pitch all these investors a big vision feels like lying to those who don't have the cushion they have to fail while losing other people's money.

Underresourced Drivers

Some people cannot be stopped.

Nothing can get in the way of their success.

These are the people who some will put up as examples when they say, "But look at this person. They did it, despite their disadvantages."

Sure, no matter what level of hardship, hard work does pay off for some people, especially with a lot of luck. It just doesn't happen for nearly enough people who come from underresourced backgrounds.

This is another piece of bad data that I really hate—that because *some* people break out of structural inequity that all it takes for everyone to do so is hard work.

That's BS.

For example, high post-incarceration rates of unemployment aren't the fault of those who were formally incarcerated who can't find work just because "some" people who were incarcerated found jobs and turned their life around.

Feeling like a driver no matter your circumstances can put a lot of pressure on yourself. If you've had the odds stacked overwhelmingly against you, your "no excuses" approach might be too much weight to bare.

Sometimes, pride makes it hard for you to accept help. The hesitance to rely on others, especially from those who are better resourced than you, can be extremely shortsighted. Everyone needs a little help once in a while. Starting a company is all about building up a team and a network of resources that you can leverage to get ahead.

A CEO can't do everything themself.

The best underresourced drivers move heaven and earth to make it work, impressing the hell out of investors, busting through the myths about who gets funded. Others crash under the pressure of trying to do it all on their own.

When these folks succeed, they'll make you feel like anything is possible, but when they end up underperforming, you'll feel even more like the system is broken, because all their hustle and grit should have gotten them a better outcome.

Resourced Passengers

For some people, starting a company feels inevitable. They do all the things they feel like they're supposed to do—go to top schools, take consulting or banking jobs, and then decide, often when getting an MBA, that starting a company and being an entrepreneur is the thing to do.

They often settle on an idea that feels a bit like a 7 out of 10—something solid but not particularly risky. There's nothing wrong with it, but it's not anything anyone gets excited about—because how could it? Their path isn't so different than anyone else's, so why would their idea be special?

Because they're well resourced, they have a nice résumé and sound smart, but they're not breaking any eggs along the way. They follow a lot of rules and things go okay, but not great. At some point, they'll run into the fact that their company just doesn't make the cut because it never breaks out—even after a small round of funding, which didn't come easy either.

They won't be able to figure out why investors aren't excited and because they feel like life happens to them. They'll inevitably blame investors for being shortsighted, or biased, or the cycle, or customers for taking too long, or anyone else but themselves.

They often have the kind of network to land on their feet—often joining the other side as investors, or in some kind of visible leadership position where they're aiming to help new founders. Inevitably, those who aren't straight white guys end up parroting the same statistics about who the system works for and who doesn't, when in reality, their idea was never top tier nor was their ability to raise.

Underresourced Passengers

You've got an idea, but you're waiting for investors to tell you whether it's good or not—and you feel lucky that they even made time for you given what you hear about who gets capital. You haven't strived to build your network among really accomplished folks because you always get caught up in "Why would they ever want to meet with me? What could I possibly offer them?"

How is it possible that you even decided to be a founder? You probably found your current career to be a bit of a dead end and you have an idealistic view of what it would be like if you got "chosen"—like the winners on *Shark Tank*. You'd like to be your own boss, if only someone would give you a shot.

Over time, because you're going through the typical channels, filling out forms on investor websites, applying to angel groups, trying business plan competitions, you're feeling like it's not going to happen. Similar to your well-resourced passenger counterparts, you'll feel like it's the fault of investors and the system—because of their bias or unfamiliarity with the area you were building in.

You'll feel bitter about the experience and a bit hopeless—and it will probably be the only thing you try to start.

I've seen founders in every quadrant succeed—and fail.

What makes the difference usually isn't the idea. It's self-awareness, clarity, and the willingness to do the unglamorous work of building relationships, asking for help, and getting back up when the world says no.

You may not control the rules of the game, but you can control how well you play your hand.

Level Setting and the Fundability Scorecard

Before we dive into Chapter 2, I think it's good context for you to level set where you are.

That's one of the hardest things to do in fundraising. VCs don't give you much feedback, so when you get passed on, you don't know if you're a solid 7 or a "can't get you out of the room fast enough" 2.

The truth is, there's no single objective way to measure the "fundability" of your startup. The decision to fund a company is a combination of a lot of human factors—an assessment of one group of humans by another group of humans, fraught with apples-to-oranges comparisons.

Yet, everyone has an opinion about how a company measures up—especially the founder. So how do you know what truth is?

Think of it like proving your identity. You need some from column A, some from column B. A driver's license counts for two points. A passport counts for four. A utility bill only counts for one. No single piece does the job on its own, but stack enough together and you pass the check.

The same is true in fundraising. Certain attributes don't buy you much upside, but their absence really hurts you. Others can tip the scales dramatically. Some are just unfair advantages—like being a known quantity to the investor.

Not all attributes carry the same weight. Some have heavy downside if you're missing them but don't add much upside if you have them. Others are rocket boosters when you've got them but don't count against you if you don't. A few are only downside, or only upside.

Figure 1.3 shows how they tend to impact your chances of raising.

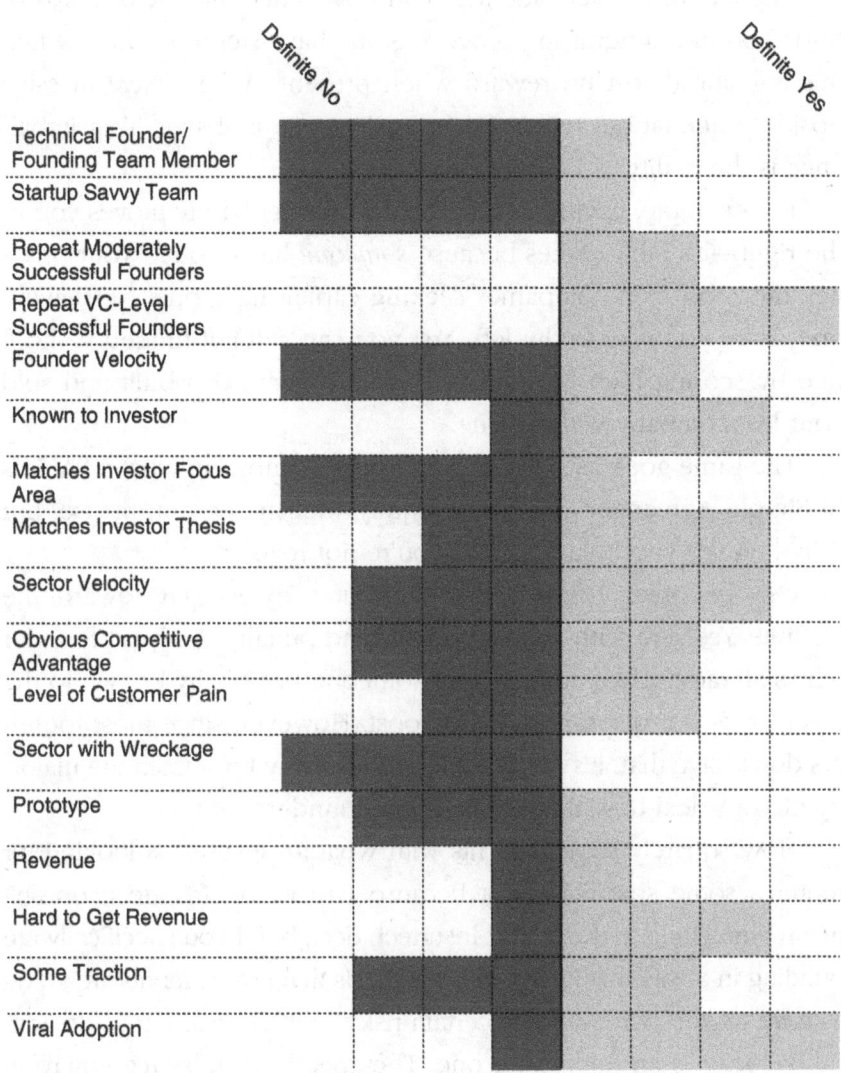

Figure 1.3 Startup Fundability Chart

If you're looking at Figure 1.3, you'll notice that every attribute sits on a horizontal bar ranging from Definite No on the left to Definite Yes on the right. But unlike a symmetric scorecard, the bars aren't all centered. Some stretch much farther in one direction than the other. That's intentional.

The length of each side tells you how much that factor helps or hurts you in a fundraising process. Some have steep penalties when missing but almost no reward when present—others have massive upside potential but barely count against you if absent. That imbalance is the reality of how investors think.

For example, having a technical co-founder barely moves you to the right—it's table stakes because *someone* has to build your product and most tech companies seeking capital have one. Not having one drags you way to the left. Yet, you can still get funded without one by scoring high in other categories. Maybe you built and sold your last company without one.

The same goes for basic startup fluency: knowing what a SAFE is (a Simple Agreement for Future Equity) doesn't earn applause, but fumbling the vocabulary signals you're not ready.

On the other hand, certain attributes extend far toward the Definite Yes side with almost no left-hand penalty. A repeat founder who's already sold a company, or someone personally known to the investor, gets a disproportionate boost. However, since most founders don't have that, it's hard to take points away for it from the majority of your deal flow that are first-time founders.

How squarely something fits with what an investor is looking for requires some specificity. Just because I focus on Insurtech doesn't mean I'm willing to do "every" Insurtech deal, but if you specifically are building in a way that aligns with my thesis that governments are going to have to start backstopping certain risks, then I'm leaning in already.

Velocity is an interesting one. The speed of the space you're in counts as equally positive or negative—but the speed you're moving as a team counts double on the downside. In other words, it's good that you're moving fast, but it's kind of expected.

If you're moving too cautiously, you're toast.

Having a prototype has become table stakes these days—especially in a world where you can vibe code (using AI) your way to almost any basic app. Not having anything to show is a lot of points off.

Revenue is a tricky one—having some of it doesn't buy you nearly as many points as you would assume. Having difficult-to-get revenue, however, like a contract with a school district if you're an edtech company, counts for a lot.

A "sector with wreckage" lives deep in the gray toward No territory, with little chance to earn its way out. Conversely, "viral adoption" lives on the opposite end—pure upside. Nobody expects you to have it, but if you do, it outweighs almost everything else.

What the grayscale makes clear is that fundability isn't binary. You're not building one perfect résumé of checkboxes. You're assembling a pattern of strengths that outweigh the inevitable weaknesses. Your job isn't to fill the whole chart in dark gray on the right—it's to understand which parts matter most, which ones you can fix, and which you simply need to offset somewhere else.

The point isn't to tally up a numeric score—it's to understand where you're strong, where you're weak, and how you should talk about each.

- ☑ Fix what you can (e.g., hire the missing technical founder).
- ☑ Frame weaknesses in context (e.g., small revenue, but from the hardest customers).
- ☑ Acknowledge the unfair ones (e.g., tough sector history) and overcompensate elsewhere.

You don't need to pick up all the possible points to get funded, but you do need enough points in the end to clear the bar.

Chapter 2

Show Me the Money

Who Gets Funded and Why?

Founders hear a lot about fundraising—what VCs look for, the magic words to say in a pitch, and who gets funded. It's not only overwhelming but also conflicting. I'd like to help you cut through some of the noise and understand how the VC funding machine works. Only then can you make it work for you.

Soul-Crushing Numbers

I'm going to start by breaking down one of the most often quoted stats out there:

> *"Only 2% of venture capital goes to women."*

That may or may not be relevant to you personally—but understanding the factors around it will help you filter and decode lots of other things you hear about venture, no matter what your background.

Think of it like writing a book about relationships by starting out with an in-depth discussion and breakdown of the widely quoted "50% of all marriages end in divorce" statistic.

You might not even be married, but you could still benefit from an exploration of why people stay together, split apart, and why people focus much more on this negative extrapolation rather than the fact that the median marriage lasts around 20 years.

The 2% number for capital going to women is shocking—and it should be to both men and women. It certainly makes the whole asset class feel like an insider's game. Even for guys, if you're not part of an "Old Boys Club" I'd imagine that this could sound a bit discouraging.

It's also . . . misleading.

That figure refers to the percentage of *all venture capital*—from pre-seed to billion-dollar growth rounds—that goes to teams with female-*only* founders.

It's not the same as the money that female CEOs raise, nor does it solely refer to the experience of people raising their *first* rounds.

Teams led by a female CEO, which include mixed founding teams of both men and women as well as female-only founding teams, raise much more. When you focus that number on pre-seed and seed rounds, they raise almost 10 times as much—closer to 20%.

That might not sound like a big percentage overall, but when something so widely circulated is off by a factor of 10, you must ask what else is said about venture capital that might be off?

It's been said that those female CEOs *needed* a male cofounder to raise, but that doesn't hold water with me. I think it takes away the accomplishments of female CEOs who raised.

Plus, only 1–2% of companies raise venture at all. If VCs just wanted the "next best set of dudes," they have plenty to choose from.

So why are the numbers so skewed, and what does that mean for your chances as a founder—regardless of your gender? Why are the numbers even worse for other underrepresented groups, such as Black founders and other founders of color?

Let's start with one of the most basic attributes of the startup funding world: most of what venture capitalists fund is tech, while most new businesses aren't tech.

By number, most new businesses are service businesses, retail shops, consumer products—small businesses run for profit and not for growth. All of these types of "Main Street" businesses require either more humans to do more business, or more physical inputs. It's hard for them to take off and grow rapidly because things like hiring, manufacturing, and needing real estate complicates things and slows growth down.

High growth is a necessary ingredient for the kind of returns that venture capitalists and other startup investors look for. Is it possible your beverage company becomes the next Liquid Death, doing over $100 million in sales in just its fourth year?

Sure.

Is that the trajectory of most beverage startups? Definitely not.

Apps can go viral. Software can be paid for and used by anyone with a computer. Anyone doing something that isn't really tech is going to need to justify how software style growth is possible, because that's what investors will compare you with.

There are lots of good business ideas out there that aren't tech, but they usually aren't the same level of *growth* opportunity.

Given that, the flows of who gets venture capital funding are highly affected by where technical talent is, and there's a huge disparity in the issuance of technical degrees. Women earn just 20% of computer science degrees. This is more than what it had been decades ago—even though women are now outlearning men in their capture of other advanced degrees.

The share of women in computer science (CS) dropped sharply after the 1980s due to a mix of cultural and educational shifts—personal computers were marketed almost exclusively to boys, creating an early experience gap. As CS programs began assuming prior exposure, women without that background were often weeded out, while pop culture reinforced the stereotype of programming as a male domain.

The tech industry itself was often an unwelcoming, even hostile, place for women, further discouraging entry and persistence. The result was a steep decline in women seeking out the degrees that would put them in this industry that bottomed out in the 2010s.

It's true that you don't need a CS degree to be an engineer, it's a useful proxy for the talent pipeline, especially since the self-taught route is even harder for women. Working men statistically have more free time. Some estimates put women's extra domestic load, including childcare, at 14 hours a week.

Given that:

1. Male founders are more likely to be technical because the technical talent pool skews heavily male.
2. Female founders, being statistically less likely to be technical, are more likely to hire a technical co-founder—who, for reason #1, is likely to be male.

This isn't about women "needing" a man for credibility. It's about the reality of the current technical talent pool. If two founders are starting a tech company, you'd expect at least one of them to be technical, which means the chances of both founders being female is only 9% (20% female technical talent × 47% female presence in the workforce), and that's before accounting for any other factors.

When I say "technical," I mean actually building the thing—writing code, designing chips—not just understanding how it works or managing a tech team. My wife learned to code faster than I ever could—but she's part of a minority in a field still overwhelmingly male.

We can take that issue seriously while acknowledging that the "2%" makes it sound like the 47% of the workforce that is female is locked out of venture in a way that is highly misleading.

The truth is more complex: female CEOs are getting funded—often against overwhelming competition from all-male teams. But the pipeline is constrained: fewer women in technical roles, heavier domestic loads, and lower average net worth (which we'll discuss the impact of in a moment) shrink the pool before the pitch meeting even happens.

Does this mean that bias doesn't exist in the process and the everyday experience of women and founders of color?

No, it 100% does.

The Hard Thing About Biased and Hard Things

Fundraising is hard for everyone—but if you're not a straight white guy, it can feel like the odds are stacked against you from the start.

A few years ago, I did something simple with my Monday morning NYC tech newsletter. On Martin Luther King Day, instead of posting something about it, I just listened. I asked Black members of the tech community to share their experiences of working in this sector.

One Black founder shared how even their last name—"Youngblood"—was questioned on a networking app, assumed to be a gang reference. That's the kind of microaggression founders of color deal with constantly—having to explain themselves just to be seen as credible.

That kind of dismissal isn't just frustrating—it's exhausting. Another founder described what it's like to be the only Black person in a 70-person tech office:

> *"Every interaction isn't just about me—it's about how I might shape someone's perception of all Black people."*

That's a burden most white founders never carry into a pitch meeting.

For women, the tax feels like a credibility penalty. Studies have shown that pitches by men are seen as more "persuasive," "fact based," and "logical." Meanwhile female founders are more likely to be asked "prevention" questions (focused on risk and losses). Male founders are asked "promotion" questions (focused on growth and upside).

Bias in venture is real, but we can't blame it for every "no." Racism, misogyny, and systematic issues exist, but they are not the *only* reasons why the funding is where it is. We can't ignore factors that might actually be in our control, or ones worth pushing on to improve equality and capital access.

When I was actively investing, I would see about 2,000 investment opportunities per year. Of those, I took about 150 first-time pitch meetings, which squares with industry averages.

The 10 deals that I funded per year (which was a lot for VC standards), represented only 0.5% of all the deals I saw.

Therefore, 99.5% of all the founders who pitched me got turned down.

I've turned down white male founders who had a prior exit for hundreds of millions of dollars and I've passed on Black female college students who had never met an investor before.

There's no doubt in my mind that the white guys thought I was crazy—a complete idiot for passing on their can't-miss idea, especially given their track record. (*Pro tip: Investors will always hear about how you badmouthed them after a pass.*)

The Black female founders had a kind of rejection fatigue. Many have explained to me that they didn't seriously believe this process was ever going to work for them.

Whether it's true or not that who you are defines your chances, it does you and your startup no good to believe that. You have to go in with the confidence of that team of rich white male founders and believe that anyone who passes on you is going to feel like a schmuck one day.

Otherwise, why try—especially when you know that two-thirds of new businesses fail and 75% of venture-backed companies fail to return investor capital?

You're willing to try to beat one set of odds, why not attempt to beat the other?

If you want to improve your chances, you need to understand not just who gets funded, but who's pitching, what venture demands, and how it works as a financial product.

The Other Side of the Table

Getting a check from a professional investor is more likely than winning the lottery, but it may not feel like it. The hard part for founders is that when you to get excited enough about an idea to decide to start working on it, you probably feel extremely confident.

All founders do—at least early on—so when fundraising is a struggle, it can't be you and your amazing idea that is the problem.

It must be the investors, right?

"They aren't familiar with my space."

Ask yourself: "Am I doing a good enough job explaining the opportunity?"

"They wanted me to be more technical."

Is that a fair critique? Is your supporting team strong enough to accomplish your product goals?

"They don't want to invest in women."

If Melanie Perkins, co-founder of Canva, pitched, would they really not back her?

Yes, investors are biased. They make assumptions about you when you walk in the door based on how you look and who you are.

You do it to them too.

Here's a secret: every single investor, despite all their biases and assumptions, is rooting for you.

When they open your email, meet you in an elevator, or hear your pitch, they're hoping that yours is going to be *the one*. They're hoping that you're going to knock their socks off, that you'll be an obvious yes.

They want you to make *them* so much money that they can retire from VC and become the Ambassador to the Czech Republic, or whatever VCs do when they retire.

This book is not just about making them "feel" like you're going to be *that* deal, but also making sure that you *actually are*.

What If It's Not?

Maybe your idea is the one—but also maybe it's not and it needs more work. Maybe five years from now you're going to come up with a much better idea. Saying this reminds me of my three-year-old daughter's running races in the park with her little friends. She's quite fast, but she doesn't always win. I remind her of that anytime they race—that she might not win.

I don't do it to be discouraging—quite the opposite. I remind her of it so that when she doesn't win, it's just a temporary setback and not a crushing loss. I also promise her the support she needs to be faster the next time—maybe not faster than all the kids, but certainly faster than the last time she raced. Whatever she wants that I can provide—healthy nutrition, good running shoes, and lots of patient practice, I'm there for her.

I just won't blow smoke at her and tell her she's the fastest kid—tying her own sense of self to always winning.

You're going to be better at this if you know that you can get beat—and that the way to lessen the chance of that is to prepare better and work on your weaknesses.

I worry a lot about founders that are working on companies in such a way there they literally cannot withstand a loss.

These include founders from cultures where failure isn't tolerated. They include founders who feel like they're at the age where this is their last shot. Maybe they're looking to prove something to someone besides themselves. I'll also include founders who have set themselves up financially where a loss on this startup would be a financial catastrophe.

These are founders who are unable to see when they're not winning and that's going to make them unable to improve or start over when the board is flashing yellow warning lights.

My hope is to get you so comfortable with admitting when something is going wrong or needs to be fixed that you become the fastest learner out there, which will actually make you a great founder.

Want to Make a Million? Start with Two Million and Lose Half of It

Let's think about venture capital as a product—because that's actually what it is. It's a financial product and founders are the target market. But is it a good product for all founders? If not, maybe we shouldn't assume all founders even want it equally.

If you're funding a business with venture capital dollars, you need to spend a lot of your prime earning years working for peanuts on something that has a statistically significant chance of earning you a whole lot of nothing in the end.

(I could write a whole different book about the psychology of why anyone would attempt something so crazy. Let's just say you founders are *built different*, to put it nicely.)

Sure, if it hits, it hits big, but the majority of startups won't return anything to anyone. You have to ask yourself who can actually afford that level of failure.

Rich people. That's who—or at least "very" comfortable people.

If you already have a nest egg, or your family does, or hell, even if you're not "that" rich, you have to be at least a little privileged if working on a startup for a few years doesn't cause significant financial or housing instability.

Two-thirds of adults can't even afford an unexpected $500 expense—so how are they supposed to afford taking this kid of big swing for the fences with their career with such a huge risk of a strikeout? Some founders are ignoring the potential of this zero outcome and the potential stability they're forgoing—but they shouldn't, especially if they have family and other dependents counting on them.

Jewel Burks Solomon is a venture capitalist. She's also a Black female and a former entrepreneur who sold her company, Partpic, to Amazon. It wasn't a billion-dollar outcome, but it was enough for her to buy a house for herself and also for her parents, who had never owned one. In a world where the median white household has approximately 10 times the wealth of the median Black household, going from renters to homeowners is a huge difference.

She's the first person who brought this idea up to me—that VC as a financial product isn't a very good fit for someone who, smartly, has a lower risk tolerance based on their current level of wealth. That's why her fund, Collab Capital uses a unique hybrid funding model called the SPACE agreement, combining equity with a revenue-sharing component. This structure allows founders to access capital while retaining more control, and includes the option to buy back equity over time.

So, while we all know bias exists in the business world, we have to consider whether or not some founders are making the perfectly rational economic decision to avoid venture capital until they can afford the risk.

And when systemic inequality has shaped who can afford to take that risk, it's worth asking how venture could evolve—not just to be more inclusive, but to offer more models that work for more people.

Alternatively, some founders want to own and control their companies longer, perhaps passing them on across generations.

That's the thing—we have *no idea* who is seeking venture capital and how much of it because no one measures *who* is pitching.

We know who gets the money, but I don't know of a single firm that tracks the backgrounds of every pitch email and meeting that comes through the door. That's the one number that would actually help founders figure out what their chance might be if they raised.

We also need to acknowledge that some of the most important inputs to successfully raising funding—technical backgrounds and the financial stability to take big risks—are not evenly distributed.

Who You Know Is What You Know

Another issue we need to confront is the experiential knowledge that flows through certain networks and not others—information that makes some founders better prepared and more likely to be successful than others.

I've made over 100 investments in my career, and nearly half of those went into diverse teams. I'll be the first to back up the notion that diverse founders have just as much ambition, drive, intellectual horsepower, creativity—you name it—than anyone else. In fact, you could make the argument that, because of their lack of advantages in other areas, the ones who make it to a venture pitch actually have more of these raw ingredients. They've had to in order to make it to the same destination as their straight white male counterparts.

There is, however, an advantage that some founders have over others that I hate to admit exists—but one that I would very much like to solve for.

A founder who has a handful of venture-backed friends—successful ones who have raised multiple rounds of capital and who have grown their companies through different stages—has a huge advantage over one who doesn't. This group of close connections can not only introduce them to capital but can give strong referrals based on years of shared history. It also provides a built-in set of advisors who can be called upon along the way.

It's not just capital access that helps.

In fact, I think that's only a small part of it given that you can find any number of investors attending open events, putting their emails on their websites, and allowing you to comment on thought leadership they share.

There's a lot of "access" out there if you look.

What makes a huge difference is that you can tell when a founder has a go-to set of people in their network to ask all the basic "dumb questions" (which are never really that dumb) about hiring, fundraising, deal doing, PR, etc. No one expects a founder to know all of these things at birth, but when you can go to breakfast with a close friend and say, "Explain to me how you ran your fundraising process . . ." or "Tell me how you successfully hired for a lead marketer," that means they're going to hit the ground running on every single aspect of growing their company and being a CEO. They just know what the job is supposed to be and what level they need to perform at because they've seen examples of it up close and over time. They're also going to be able to speak to what they need to do better in a fundraising pitch—coming off as a lot more capable, earning trust from investors.

Now ask yourselves the question: Who has a close-knit group of venture-backed friends?

We all know the answer to that.

Because of where venture dollars have historically flowed, and because most people's networks look like themselves, people who are well connected to other venture-backed founders are disproportionally straight white males.

The reasons why are plentiful and probably overlapping. We can argue about the why, but the fact remains true that not only are capital networks highly segregated, but so are the networks of successful founders themselves.

This has really bothered me—because as much as I believe that everyone has an equal shot at success once given the opportunity, it's hard for me to argue with the notion that these networks of success are themselves an advantage—one that is not evenly distributed.

It's also not something you can fix overnight, either. There are all sorts of well-intentioned mentoring programs, networking events, etc., that stick a bunch of people in a room once, or for a couple of meetings to help outsiders become insiders. That's different than spending two years of an MBA program together, including all the side trips, having your kids go to the same school, playing on softball teams together, etc.

It's something to think about if you think that entrepreneurship will be in your future. Ask yourself, "Am I an island?" Are you a big fish in a small pond, unique within your network, but disconnected from people who the very top level of experience doing the things that you would like to be doing? Or are you well connected—friends even—with people not only a couple of steps ahead that you, but with high levels of success who you can learn from?

This is something that everyone, no matter their background, needs to ask themselves. Am I an insider—and if I'm not, what am I missing?

"Do I know what a great pitch—one that won over investors—sounds like?"

"Have I ever seen someone fundraise successfully up close?"

"Do I have someone I can call when I'm unsure what specific clauses in a VC term sheet means?"

"How would my pitch change if I was surrounded by more people who had succeeded in raising?"

Candis Best, a Black female founder, told me that before joining the Startup Leadership Program (SLP), a startup mentoring and education program, she had no idea how disconnected she was from the insider networks and knowledge flows that make startup success possible.

She wasn't short on talent—just information access, but she didn't even realize it.

This might be a disheartening realization—but like everything else in this book, it shouldn't be. Luckily for you, despite all the terrible things that might be happening in the world at any given time, we are living in the most connected era in history. When I was in college, if I wanted to contact an alumnus from my school, I had to go to the school library to get a physical book full of alumni addresses. Only a small percentage of them even had email addresses listed.

I had to write them letters to network—like a cave person!

Now, nearly every venture professional and entrepreneur is not only on LinkedIn, but many of them are also openly sharing their knowledge and experience through social media—and even responding to comments and cold outreach.

With the sum of all entrepreneurial knowledge available on your phone in the form of Medium posts, podcasts, and even TikTok, you should feel like it's at least possible to catch up to the people who grew up around this stuff—maybe not in wealth (not yet) but in knowledge and connection.

The answers are out there.

The knowledgeable people, in my experience, are willing to answer your questions. You just have to double down on intentionally seeking it out and connecting to it so you can be that founder who seems well connected and like an insider in your pitch.

If you don't have a trusted circle of experienced founders, your number-one job—before you pitch—is to build one.

Who Are These VCs We Put on Pedestals?

Before we go into surrounding yourself with really smart people, I want to take a second to tell you how I feel about some of the venture professionals you're pitching on the other side of the table.

I have a saying: "Hell is other VCs."

I'm telling you this because I want founders to stop putting VCs on a pedestal. They should be grateful to meet you, not the other way around.

The Junior Folks

I've often said that I wouldn't want to hire anyone for a venture job who wanted a venture job. The way people see the job from the headlines—the kingmaking, getting in to all the insider spaces—it self-selects for all the wrong things you want in a partner.

Most are parroting the firm's POV, trading gossip, or making you feel like your worth depends on sneaking them into a hot deal. They look busy, but none of them can actually say yes.

They've been hired to vet whether something is a good idea, but the very best founders already know something is a great idea and wouldn't ever pitch someone junior because they can't actually help the founder.

This is one of the reasons why I coach VCs—to help upwardly mobile venture professionals figure out why someone would want to meet with them and how to genuinely offer value for a founder's time.

The ones who are actually thoughtful, independent researchers are caught between a rock in a hard place—trying hard to create a truly unique thesis when they know exactly the type of company A16Z is looking to fund downstream.

Few of them standout, most likely because of the egos of the partners of their firms—unwilling to be overshadowed by the former banker they hired to write their internal memos.

Also, everything is "we" when most have no "juice" in the firm. The general partners are usually the ones with the real pull who are sourcing the best deals.

I was this guy when I was an analyst at Union Square Ventures—except for the standing out part. Credit to Fred Wilson and Brad Burnham being egoless enough to hire someone with a big, visible personality, for better or worse.

Are there exceptions? Sure. When I was a principal at First Round Capital, I led eight deals in two years—but that was obvious to the outside. I could speak to leading those deals in public. You could ask the founders how those deals were sourced. I wasn't just "on the deal team" siphoning credit. Some very special up-and-comers are breaking through and building their own track record as junior folks.

Know which ones you're pitching with the use of direct questions.

Have you led a deal in the last six months?

Was it your deal or are you tag teaming it with a general partner?

How does the voting process work within your fund?

The Hustling Emerging Managers

Every conversation is a thinly veiled pitch for their own fund. Since they're usually raising money and investing at the same time, it's unclear which hat they're wearing when they corner you. Do you have angel investors who could be LPs in their fund? They'd love to meet them (and you, they suppose).

No one's making any money yet, but everyone's doing great and excited about their portfolio that they won't be able to cash in on for another six to eight years.

That deal that a brand-name fund just did at a crazy valuation that they missed out on? How dumb was that?

I've 100% been this guy.

They can be easier money given that they're no longer at a highly competitive brand-name firm. That is, if they actually have the money.

Make sure they're not funding you "right after they close more money from LPs."

That's going to be a long wait.

The Industry Icons

These folks aren't just celebrities anymore—they've gone full James Bond supervillain. Once upon a time, they were real innovators who built cool shit because it could be built. They were hustlers like you wanting to change the world for the better.

Now they're the loudest people in the room, posing for Oval Office photo ops, shutting down public beaches, and doling out attention to founders like they're volunteering at a soup kitchen. Forget the fact they created the food shortage—be thankful they're willing to grace you with their presence.

Now they've become billionaires playing dress-up as philosophers, using podcasts and manifestos to justify why the world should bend around them.

They talk about "freedom" and "innovation," but it always cashes out the same way: protecting their wealth.

Decentralization? Really just code for no oversight.

"Time to build"? Translation: as long as it's not in their backyard.

They rail against regulation as if it's a threat to humanity, when what they really mean is it might slow down the money printer. The irony is, for all the power they project, many of their ideas are paper-thin because they can't get out of their own filter bubble.

"Anyone who can code or who can design has 0% chance of homelessness in the U.S." is actually real sentiment that Khosla Ventures partner Keith Rabois tried to argue, all while fundamentally misunderstanding and dismissing how people become homeless and the factors around it.

Thanks to AI doing the work of entry-level coders, that tweet seems surely not to age well.

Yet they deliver them with the confidence of someone who's never been told no since their first carry check cleared. They're not here to inspire. They're here to consolidate power and remind you who owns the table you're pitching across.

Being in their orbit doesn't feel like access to brilliance—it feels like wandering into the Multiverse, where the only real superpower is compounding interest.

The Old Guys

They'll corner you to rehash the glory days—Netscape, Webvan, their loose connection to Google founders Larry and Sergei. They love to remind you how different it was "back then" and how "the fundamentals never change." The problem is, they have zero idea how today's markets work, or what it's like to raise from TikTok-famous angels.

They show up because they're bored, not because they're useful. And somehow, they still dominate the panel slots. The only thing older than they are is the money that backs them as LPs.

Dysfunctional Firms, Dysfunctional Experience

It's not just the VCs who are a bit wonky; it's entire firms!

VCs love to market themselves as world-class institutions. In reality, a lot of firms are held together with duct tape and ego. The dysfunction at the partnership level inevitably seeps into how they treat founders.

The Unequal Partnerships

At most firms, one or two partners really drive the bus. Everyone else is dead weight with carry. If you happen to win over the "wrong" partner—the one without clout, or whose last deal blew up—good luck. Your round will rot in committee while the heavyweights chase whatever shiny object they care about that week. They love to say they "decide as a partnership." Translation: nothing happens unless the dominant voices bless it, and even then, it can take weeks. Great founders slip through the cracks because the system is designed to protect politics, not surface the best opportunities.

Ironically, the only ones actually hustling—the associates and principals who are out at every demo day, on Discord servers, scraping LinkedIn—are the ones with zero power. They know what's bubbling up, but their insights get run through three layers of hierarchy until the signal is so diluted it barely resembles your pitch.

The people closest to the ground floor have the least say.

Decision Paralysis

Firms that pretend to be "consensus-driven" wind up in endless partner meetings where no one wants to stick their neck out. The result? Your round drags on while they debate whose turn it is to take risk. You're left bleeding out your runway while they polish their memos and ask for more information in the data room.

Partner Churn

That "champion" you won over? They leave the firm, and suddenly you're an orphaned portfolio company. The remaining partners have no real attachment to you—you're just another line on a cap table they didn't pick. Good luck getting mindshare after that.

Misaligned Incentives

Some firms are raising their next fund before they've even finished deploying the current one. Which means they care more about looking good in LP decks than supporting you. If your metrics don't fit their marketing narrative, you're sidelined—no matter how solid your fundamentals.

Boardroom Chaos

The dysfunction shows up most brutally when a partner brings it into the boardroom. One is trying to steer you into risky bets to juice their numbers, another is hedging and telling you to slow down, and a third is barely engaged at all. You're stuck managing their contradictions instead of building your business.

For founders, this means you're not just pitching an individual; you're inheriting the entire messy ecosystem behind them. Their firm's baggage becomes your baggage. And when you need clarity, support, or conviction, what you often get is politics, delay, and distraction.

Yes, you need their money but take them off the pedestal. When you're raising for VC, they're not sending their best.

You'll have plenty to complain about over drinks with other founders when the process is done.

Chapter 3
I'm Putting Together a Team
Attracting Help and Support

When we talk about having the right team in a startup, it's easy to assume we're only talking about employees. That feels understandably limiting for bootstrapped founders who can't afford to hire until they get more funding.

If that's the only way you think about the team behind this company, you're missing out on building a critical support system. The best early-stage companies look more like parades—with the founder leading a wide variety of supporters of the company. Some join as early employees, some as angel investors, while others are just super fans who make tons of intros and provide a lot of customer-centric feedback.

Before we talk about getting help, we have to talk about whether it's a good idea to share your idea, especially before you build it. A lot of founders are cagey about giving away the details. They're afraid someone might steal it before they get a chance to build a moat.

There are a bunch of reasons why you shouldn't be worried about this—most notably because you really can't do anything about it if it happens.

Even if someone did steal your idea, you don't really have the budget to defend it in court unless you're funded. Plus, it would be terrifically hard proving that there's no other possible way that this person didn't come up with the idea some other way. Unless you're a scientist who made an actual technical discovery after a lot of research and experimentation, you're probably not the only person who ever thought of this thing. It happens all the time that multiple people independently come up with the same idea.

In the 1890s, radio wasn't invented by a lone genius, but by at least five pioneers working independently—Marconi, Tesla, Popov, Bose, and Lodge. How is that possible? They were each building on Hertz's discovery of electromagnetic waves—an advancement that made radio possible and a somewhat obvious next step for anyone in the know.

Without knowing of each other's progress, they arrived at similar breakthroughs almost simultaneously, driven by the same tantalizing possibility of wireless communication.

The truth is, ideas rarely exist in total isolation—they emerge from the same soup of technology, culture, and unmet needs that others are swimming in too. What separates successful founders isn't secrecy. It's execution, momentum, and the relationships that accelerate both.

When you keep your idea locked up, you're not protecting it—you're starving it. Ideas need oxygen. They need testing, refining, challenging. They need believers. The very act of sharing is how you recruit the people who will help pressure-test the concept, point out blind spots, introduce your first pilot customer, or even write your first check.

Yes, there's a risk that someone hears your idea and runs with it—but what's more likely is that, if they're entrepreneurial, they're running with their own idea. It's the best idea and, to them, yours is pretty stupid. After all, isn't that what you often think about other people's pitches when you hear them?

There's a far greater risk that nobody hears it at all—and it never becomes real. Startups don't die because someone "stole the idea." They die because they never gathered enough energy, feedback, and conviction to get off the ground.

When you talk openly about what you're building, you're not just pitching an idea—you're planting a flag. You're saying, "This is the problem I care about. If you care too, come walk with me."

That's how the parade starts. So how do you get out there in front of the right people for this parade—especially if you're not already an insider?

The Network Upkeep Problem

Most ambitious people who have a startup idea already have a decent network—but it's one they've underutilized. By the time they figure out what they need, most of the people who can help them with it are people they haven't spoken to in ages.

I know this because I made the mistake early in my career of falling into two traps:

1. I didn't build relationships with people unless I specifically wanted to do their job or work for them in the near term.
2. When I found someone I wanted to connect with, I couldn't figure out what I had to offer them. Not only did I hesitate to reach out, but I also didn't keep up the relationship over time.

I was looking at all of these people as a means to the next job versus what they could have been:

- Sources of knowledge about business best practices and interesting problems to solve.
- Advocates of mine to others in their network who might be more relevant to the things I wanted to do than they were.
- Sources of capital—because many of these folks were successful enough to be angel or fund investors, had I spent the time building trust with them over time.

Be Curious

Here's how I would have started building my network earlier if I could have done it all over again—and how you can start right now. It starts with believing that being curious is all you need to start a conversation with someone successful.

That's how venture capitalist and popular VC podcaster Harry Stebbings started.

Today, he runs a $400 million venture capital fund, but in 2015, then 18-year-old Harry launched *The Twenty Minute VC* podcast from his bedroom in London. He had no background in venture capital. No industry connections. No podcasting experience.

Harry wanted to learn about venture capital—how investors think, what makes a great startup, why some bets pay off while others flop. Fast forward a few years, and *The Twenty Minute VC* became one of the most influential podcasts in venture capital. Harry built a brand, a network, and eventually a venture fund—not by having all the answers, but by asking great questions before he had the perfect job, a mentor, an MBA, or anything to pitch.

He cold-emailed VCs and invited them on his podcast.

Not to pitch them. Not to impress them. Just to learn from them.

Guy Kawasaki and Brad Feld were early big names who agreed to come on, but why did they bother?

You can say all you want about people being nice or willing to help out when you're coming from the right place—but I actually think Harry stumbled on a hack that a lot of people don't realize. It doesn't matter whether you have any kind of a following or not. The person you're interviewing does and so does the person you interview after that person and so on.

Having a following means you need to "feed the beast." To keep your followers engaged, you need to be interesting on a regular basis, which is really difficult.

You make it easy for them by showing up with great questions for them to answer and the willingness to edit a video or article they can use to show off how interesting they are.

Even if you don't have a following, they do. When they tag you or reshare the conversation, a few people in their network will check you out. Then the next guest does the same. You're not chasing virality. You're building surface area—giving people reasons to follow you, trust you, and see you as part of the flow of interestingness in their feed.

Being a "public student" in this way gives you borrowed credibility and distribution.

Most people try to posture as experts too early. Curiosity scales better. If you're not *the* person in a field, you're better off positioning yourself as the most tenacious learner.

How is this immediately relevant to you as a founder? Imagine you send your pitch deck to an investor and they click through to your LinkedIn profile or they Google your name. What are they going to see? Wouldn't it be better if they got a chance to see you having great, insightful conversations with the best and brightest people you've been able to connect with?

Being a founder is all about facing new challenges. When investors try to figure out if you can scale into being the CEO of a big company, they're going to have to bet on your ability to learn best practices from your network and tap them for expertise.

Why not show them you're already doing just that? You don't need credibility to start—you build credibility by starting.

Cruising Without a Destination

If you're just starting out—perhaps an ambitious student hoping to start a company one day but not sure where your interests lay—you can start out with the Venn diagram of *ikigai*, the Japanese word for "a reason for being."

You may have seen it before: a four-circle Venn combining what you love, what you're good at, what the world needs, and what you can be paid for (see Figure 3.1).

The concept isn't actually Japanese. It was created by Spanish author Andrés Zuzunaga as a "purpose" framework and later rebranded with the word ikigai. Still, the Westernized version endures because it's a simple, visual way to get people to reflect on alignment between passion, skills, service, and livelihood—a useful prompt, even if it isn't the authentic tradition.

These circles can be turned into directions for you to approach networking—especially when combined with the willingness to swing for the fences. It's what I refer to as the "11 out of 10" way to level set.

In any endeavor, where's the high bar, and how do you surpass it?

Take "what you love." Maybe you really love baseball. Well, have you ever reached out to anyone who works for your favorite team in

Figure 3.1 Ikigai

the front office? What does the business around the team look like—the media networks, the technology used to scout, analyze, and train players? Do any former players currently run interesting businesses? What do the players invest in when they hit it big?

How about "what you're good at"? If you're creative and have a little bit of marketing savvy, who's *the best* at it? Who's won awards for it? Who launched and ran marketing for the biggest startup you care about? How is the job of a marketer changing in a world of data and generative AI? How can you get even better at it?

What the world needs? That's a great question to ask just about everyone:

> *"What's the biggest hurdle to your industry operating better or benefitting more people?"*

What you can be paid for? That's another easy one to ask around:

> *"What's something you'd pay someone to help you figure out right now if you found the right person?"*

If you start pulling on these threads early, you'll realize that some of them resonate more than others—and you'll start to narrow your focus. Eventually, you're not just asking questions of anyone you meet. You're asking people who invest in real estate or builders why there's a housing problem and what their opinions are on how to solve it.

These questions help you turn vague interests into specific outreach targets.

The Flywheel

When you record these interviews and publish them (tools like Riverside make it super easy to do on your own), you're building a curiosity>thought leadership flywheel:

1. You interview a smart person.
2. You learn things and something resonates.
3. You share what resonates by processing it into some insights, which garners a following and some engagement.
4. You interview another smart person, asking even more insightful questions based on prior interviews.
5. You share again, earning more followers and more engagement.
6. Your insights level up and you become knowledgeable enough to be worth interviewing yourself.
7. Never stop sharing and learning—building audience in the process.

The never stop sharing part is where regular email updates come in handy.

Networking is a long game, and most people play it badly. They either show up only when they need something or they disappear into the ether, hoping people will somehow remember them when it matters. The truth is: if you're not maintaining your presence in people's minds, you're not in their lives.

That matters, because everyone has limited slots they can keep in meaningful orbit.

It's a concept from British anthropologist Robin Dunbar, who suggested that humans can only maintain about 150 meaningful social relationships at once. It's not just about remembering names—it's about the cognitive and emotional capacity to actually keep track of people's lives in a way that feels real. Once you're in someone's Dunbar circle, you're part of the group they naturally think of when opportunities, ideas, or introductions come up.

The Heartbeat Habit

Want to stay top of mind? Send a direct email on a regular basis to your network—a **Heartbeat Email**.

Think of it as a lightweight but consistent way to remind people you exist as a full human being—not just a LinkedIn title or a profile photo. It's the rhythm that keeps you connected without the impossible logistics of 100 coffee chats a year.

We're not talking about a transactional company update that treats everyone like a potential investor. Obviously, when you start and run a company, you'll discuss what's going on, but you're more than just a founder and your recipients are more than just checkbooks.

Why It Works

We remember people who are vivid. Someone who only pings you with a press release about their company isn't memorable. But the founder who shares that she's raising her Series A and also learning to bake sourdough with her kid? That person sticks in your head. The CRO whose six-year-old just painted his nails? You're not going to forget the story of how it landed him an enterprise deal.

A Heartbeat Email makes you more than your job—it's the combination of wins, struggles, quirks, and reflections that turn you into a real person worth rooting for.

Who to Send It To

Start with anyone you'd grab coffee with if time and geography were unlimited: mentors, peers, collaborators, and friends who cheer for you. Don't overthink it—the right recipients are people who would actually be glad to get an update from you.

Don't worry about reaching a bit either. Add people you'd love to work with or build a better connection with who know you but that youd like to be closer to.

Worse comes to worse they just unsubscribe. (I use a tool called Gmail Merge by Digital Inspiration. It sends like a separate email, as opposed to a Mailchimp or Substack, but you can add in unsubscribe links.)

How to Structure It

A good cadence is monthly or quarterly. The structure is simple:

- *Greeting*—Keep it warm. Mention the season or something small that grounds the note in time.
- *Professional Update*—What you're working on, celebrating, or struggling with. Not just the highlight reel—humans bond over challenges too.
- *Personal Note*—Share a glimpse outside of work: training for a triathlon, teaching your kid chess, bingeing on a new hobby. These details are sticky.
- *Reflection*—A thought, idea, or lesson you're chewing on—maybe something you've read. People love to hear what's rattling around in your head.
- *Engagement*—Is there an event coming up, a resource you're looking for, or a question you want answered? Maybe you'll be "coming to a city near you." Give them a hook.
- *Closing*—Keep it light, grateful, and open-ended.

Style Matters

The tone should be conversational, warm, and unmistakably you. If it feels like a corporate newsletter, you've missed the point.

Err on the side of human. A few paragraphs is plenty—respect people's time while giving them something real.

The Payoff

Heartbeat Emails make you hard to forget. They position you as a three-dimensional character in someone else's story, not just a two-line entry in their contacts app. Over time, you'll find that people introduce you more, think of you more, and reach out more. And when the moment comes that you do need something—an intro, advice, support—you won't feel like you're reaching out cold.

Direct emails to your network are also a great solution for people who feel like posting on social media is a bit narcissistic for them. If you're not the grandstanding type, curating an email list of people you know well and want to hear back on may seem like a better fit. Of course, this won't make you as discoverable, but it could be a great start and a way to get comfortable with writing and sharing.

Whatever channel you choose to share, you might find that this cycle of asking good questions, talking to interesting and accomplished people, and sharing what you've learned takes on a life of its own.

Planeteer Capital founder Sophie Purdom, for example, built her reputation around her Climate Tech VC newsletter, which started as a way to organize her own thoughts and updates for peers in the climate space. By writing in her own voice—curious, pragmatic, and a little contrarian—she didn't just share information, she gave people a lens through which to see the industry.

That's what regular thought leadership does. You start being the person people think of when something new is happening in your category.

Sophie's regular cadence and multidimensional perspective made her an indispensable node in the climate tech network, setting her up to launch a new $50 million fund, convene events, and influence where capital flows.

Brad Hargreaves did something similar in real estate and proptech through his Thesis Driven newsletter. By consistently distilling what was happening in housing, zoning, and the future of cities, Brad positioned himself not just as a founder but as a thoughtful guide through an industry in flux. His smart, digestible takes that blended policy, design, and technology. This translated into access, opportunities, and the credibility to experiment with new ideas.

It also formed the heart of a bootstrapped business that makes millions of dollars in recurring revenue per month.

Together, Sophie and Brad show how regular communication can push you past the flat LinkedIn version of yourself. By writing consistently and with personality, they made thousands of readers to trust their instincts and insight.

When you add a bit of just being human, you get three-dimensional memorability is the secret ingredient that positions you to lead, influence, and innovate.

Accomplish this and you'll go from an unknown starting from a position of zero trust with an investor to someone generating inbounds from VCs who get the hint from your posting, writing, and videos that you're working on something interesting. When they're following you for your insights, you move closer and closer to being a "blank check" team that anyone would back if they had the chance.

Roster Construction: How to Build a Team

There's no "I" in startup.

One of the toughest things you'll need to do as a founder is hire—and it's one of the essential skills that investors will judge you on, even if you never talk about it in a pitch meeting.

When you're sitting across from someone, they're wondering whether you're going to be able to return hundreds of millions to their fund.

This doesn't happen unless you "build a big company" and big companies are full of a lot of people—people who you'll need to recruit. A founder is going to be directly responsible for at least the first 50 or so hires before they get help.

Yet, recruiting is ridiculously hard and even harder for an early-stage startup.

Think of what it takes to convince a startup employee to sign on.

When a venture fund invests in you, they're diversified—you're one of 30 or 40 bets in a portfolio. If things don't work out, they can absorb the loss.

An employee, on the other hand, makes one big bet every time they join a company. If it blows up in six months, they're left with a hole in their résumé and a lot of regret.

That risk feels enormous.

Add to that the fact that you can't pay what Google, Meta, or OpenAI pay, and you're already starting at a disadvantage.

Investors know that no matter how good your idea is, you won't get far without the network and the skill to build a great team, so proving that you can as early as possible will help your case for gaining investment.

Here's the good news: proving you can recruit doesn't actually take money. In fact, the process can make your pitch and your company stronger before you've hired a single person.

Finding a Co-Founder

Let's start with the co-founder question: "Do you really need one?"

No, you don't, but a really great one is invaluable and will increase your chance of success. Investors know this, so they're more likely to back two great founders than just one.

First off, no one has "all" the skills necessary to start a company. You're always going to need a team that complements you, so why not start from the very first person to join you? Having a partner who brings different skills to the table, shares the emotional load, and helps shoulder the risk can make the journey less lonely and more resilient.

The more relevant question is whether or not the second person into the company should be employee number one or an actual co-founder.

A co-founder is taking existential risk with you. They're putting their career, finances, and often reputation on the line in exchange for a meaningful ownership stake. The bet is binary: if the company fails, their equity is worthless. Employee number one is taking a job. They're still taking on more risk than someone who joins later, but they expect to be compensated primarily in salary, with equity as upside rather than as the whole pie.

A co-founder helps define what the company is—the mission, culture, strategy, and early product direction. They're part of the "why" and "what." Employee number one is focused more on the "how." They execute, build, and shape things inside a vision that's already been set.

A co-founder is someone you could imagine running the company if you get hit by a bus.

Co-founders make foundational choices together: who to raise from, what markets to pursue, how to structure equity, what the values are. Employees weigh in, but they don't co-own those calls. Employee number one might build the first version of the product or run the first sales calls, but they're not deciding whether to pivot or sell the company.

Co-founders typically split a double-digit share of the company between them (20–50% each depending on the setup). Employee number one's grant is usually in the low single digits at most, even if they're incredibly impactful. That difference reflects governance, voting rights, and long-term wealth potential.

A co-founder is presumed to be there for the full ride—through the messiness of zero to one and ideally into scale. Interestingly enough, many of them don't make it, because they don't find a specific role to focus on and lead out of the many balls they might have in the air on day one. Still, you want someone in there who you hope can be there at the end when you ring the bell at the stock exchange.

Employee number one might not last forever, and that's fine. They could help get you to product-market fit and then leave, or transition out once the company grows beyond their sweet spot. A co-founder "quitting" feels like a crisis.

An early employee moving on is just part of company life.

So how do you find a co-founder?

First of all, you shouldn't force the issue. If you do want one, you should be intentional about it. A co-founder is a multiplier if you're aligned, but a time bomb if you're not. Too many people pick someone based on proximity—you already knew this person and they also happened to want to start a company at the same time.

"Hey, we're both single! Let's get married" probably has an equally high chance of success as choosing a co-founder this way.

All icky implications aside, finding a co-founder is closer to dating than hiring. Timing rarely lines up, risk tolerance isn't equal, and the person you loved shipping with inside a big company may be a terrible fit for zero-to-one chaos.

Treat it like a process and don't settle (in either co-founder matching or dating). You're not hunting for chemistry alone; you're testing for judgment, ownership, and stamina under stress.

Start with deliberate sourcing and fast disqualification. Tap communities where builders actually congregate, ask for targeted intros, and run a couple of short conversations to surface quick "no's" on ambition, funding philosophy, and lifestyle realities. Then stop theorizing and do a two-week trial.

Whiteboard or build together—but whatever you do, if you do start working in any small way with someone, make sure you have even a lightweight agreement on whether the person is owed anything for their work.

For consumer ideas, ship the smallest ugly thing you can and watch what happens. For enterprise, run a real discovery sprint: 10 customer calls, written notes, and a go/no-go. The work reveals more about fit than any coffee chat ever will.

Layer in a structured alignment test.

AI can create for you a short questionnaire about values, roles, equity philosophy, governance, decision rights, and a "how I behave when I'm at my worst." Compare answers across a few working sessions. Keep nonnegotiables brutally short—table-stakes skills, judgment when you're not in the room, and basic maturity.

Expect drop-offs and make them clean. Most pairings won't survive the prototype phase.

Good.

Set explicit go/no-go dates, part amicably, and preserve the relationship. Many "no's" become referrals or early hires later. The trap to watch is runway. You should give this search the same seriousness you'd give an executive hire, but be honest about your clock so you don't grab the nearest warm body in month five.

Eventually, you stop optimizing for more data and decide. The bar isn't perfection—it's enough trust and alignment to hand each other real ownership and keep investing in the relationship after the ink is dry. Treat co-founder health as an operating priority with recurring check-ins, not a vibe you hope persists.

Get this right and recruiting, speed, and culture all compound. Get it wrong and nothing you do next will move the needle. If it doesn't work out, move on sooner than later. That's why co-founders should have vesting relationships where you don't earn equity unless you work a minimum amount of time for the company (usually a minimum of a year).

Once you've got the right person, then you can move on to the rest of the org chart. It should be known that not all co-founders join at the very beginning of a company. You could make a few hires to start building your product, get some traction, and then bring in a co-founder a bit later when you're leveling up the complexity of the company by raising money, going to market, etc. In other words, you don't automatically earn the right to be called a co-founder by being there at the beginning, nor do you have to be there at the beginning to earn a co-founder title.

Finding the Right Mix of Employees Within Your Budget

> "... Of the 20,000 notable players for us to consider, I believe that there is a championship team ... of 25 people that we can afford, because everyone else in baseball undervalues them. Like ... an island of misfit toys."
>
> —**Peter Brand, played by Jonah Hill, in Moneyball (2011)**

Lay out the people needs of the company for your first two years. Forget whether you have the budget today. Just design the team that would be ideal for your stage and your ability to manage.

A technical founder can't realistically hire 30 engineers on day one. You couldn't onboard them and you couldn't build a culture. You would drown in complexity.

Be realistic, and base hiring milestones on triggers, not calendars:

- Hire sales once the product is stable and customer-ready.
- Bring in back-end scaling talent once you actually have customer load.

- Hire for full-time marketing positions when you've found proof of product-market fit.

This is how you align the build-out of your team with the real needs of the business.

Pressure-Test Your Plan

Once you've sketched out your ideal hires, test it with people who've been there. Ask a founder who has built a sales team whether your timeline and expectations make sense. Ask an engineering leader whether your hiring ratios are realistic. Run it by investors who've watched dozens of companies grow.

Don't ask generically—go function by function with people who've lived it. This process not only improves your plan, it also signals to investors that you're approaching team-building with discipline and humility.

You Wouldn't Happen to Know Anyone Who Wants to Get Rich at This Startup with Your Exact Skillset, Would You?

Here's the real hack: you can start recruiting before you can afford anyone.

When you meet someone who could one day be your head of sales, don't pitch them a job you can't pay for yet. Walk them through your product, ask whether your assumptions on sales cycles are realistic, and get them excited about the opportunity. They'll vet your plan, you'll vet their expertise. Meanwhile you're building a relationship.

If you keep these conversations alive with a steady drip of progress updates, by the time you do have the money, they're already primed to join. Investors love to see this legwork—it shows motion.

No one wants to hop on a train sitting idle at the station only to see it wait around for another hour.

Don't Pre-Reject Yourself

A lot of founders talk themselves out of outreach because they assume nobody will talk to them without money in hand. That's the wrong mindset. The truth is, you don't know where someone is in their career.

Maybe they've saved enough to take a risk. Maybe they're burned out at Big Tech. Maybe they'll say no but recommend you to the perfect candidate later.

Hiring is a funnel. You'll need to talk to a hundred people to make that first great hire. Each conversation—even the ones that don't go anywhere—increases your surface area for luck.

Be Careful with Equity

One final warning: don't confuse equity with free currency. Giving a big slug of stock to a first developer just to get an MVP built can look cheap now, but if you're pitching VCs on a billion-dollar outcome, you may have effectively paid that early developer $100 million. That's the most expensive code you'll ever buy.

Instead, think creatively. Sometimes the most senior, expensive leader isn't right for day one anyway.

Hack: The Pro + Rookie Model

You don't need a $300,000 VP on payroll to get VP-level outcomes. Pair one seasoned "pro" with one or two hungry "rookies." The pro lends judgment, playbooks, and taste; the rookies supply time, energy, and iteration. It's the startup version of a veteran athlete coaching up first-years.

Why It Works

- **Comp arbitrage:** You buy great judgment by the hour for just the time it takes to create it, not for the time it takes to execute on it.
- **Faster learning loops:** Juniors execute. The pro prevents obvious dead-ends.
- **Investor signaling:** You show "adult supervision" and experience without the Series-B burn.

How to Run It

- **Roster:** 1 fractional pro (2–4 hours/week) + 1–2 junior hires (20–40 hours/week).
- **Cadence:** Weekly working session + limited office hours.
- **Scope:** Tie the pro's involvement to one lane (sales, business development, or marketing) and one clear KPI.

Examples

- **Sales:** Pro creates Initial Customer Profiles, talk tracks, and objection maps; rookies do the prospecting.
- **Engineering:** Pro sets branching strategy, code review rules, and reliability standards; rookies ship slices of the product.
- **Marketing:** Pro defines positioning and messaging pillars; rookies run content and distribution.

Comp Guardrails

- Fractional pro: $200–500/hour and/or a small advisor grant (0.1–0.35%).
- Paper it cleanly: scope, hours cap, and conflict checks.

When investors ask, "How will you build the team?" you can answer with specifics:

> "Our fractional CRO designed the talk tracks; two juniors are hitting 40 touches a day, generating three SQOs a week. Cycle time is 41 days, win rate 17% and rising. We'll convert to a full-time sales lead once we hit 12 logos and $40,000 MRR."

I love it when a plan comes together.

The Hiring Checklist

- ☐ Draft a two-year hiring blueprint, based on triggers not calendars.
- ☐ Pressure-test it with experienced operators function by function.
- ☐ Start relationship-building with potential hires before you have cash.
- ☐ Keep your hiring funnel wide—100 convos for one great hire.
- ☐ Protect equity: don't overspend stock on "cheap" help.
- ☐ Use the Pro+Rookie model to get leverage without breaking the bank.

No *Bored* Meetings

Before you hire anyone, raise capital, or even file an LLC, create structure. Moving from idea to reality requires a way to test hypotheses and get honest feedback on what's working and what's not. That means feedback loops, accountability, and regular, high-quality input.

Traditional boards usually arrive after equity financing—which could be years in. You might spend a year of nights and weekends, another year on a SAFE, and even then your seed investors may not take a seat. You could be three years in before you have a real board.

That's a long time to fly solo—even if you have a co-founder, who may be drinking the same Kool-Aid as you do.

I suggest a "Board Before the Board"—a lightweight, informal version of the real thing that gives founders the structure they need without the overhead. Meeting monthly with a few trusted people can create the right kind of structure (and a little bit of pressure) to move forward.

Who should be on this?

This isn't the time for getting someone who just looks impressive in a pitch deck but doesn't have the time to be helpful. Nor should you tie it to how much money someone has put in. This is a *working* group meant to help you reach your early-stage goals.

Ideally, you want a mix of perspectives around the room—diverse across experience as well as demographics if you can. As an investor, I never thought I had all the right ideas (a rare admission for a VC, I know!) and very much appreciated hearing other people's take. Plus, it's a more powerful signal when multiple people can get on the same page. This is more likely to happen when everyone is in the same room—a productive contrast to getting eight different perspectives from eight different people you sit and have coffee with individually.

Here are the personas of what I think would make a great three person "pre-board":

The Business Modeler

Not just someone good with numbers, this person is familiar with lots of different types of businesses and how they work. Part CFO, part mad scientist, they'll full of creative solutions that actually pencil out. They might ask why matchmakers might not also charge for a full datability evaluation, or why you can't pay into a higher tier of the singles database. The workout challenge app that only charges people if they "don't" keep their streak going? That was their creative financial suggestion.

The Insider

This person is the voice of your customer in the room. In fact, they probably will be a consumer once you build this—and they know plenty of others they can introduce you to. In fact, they're speaking at the most important industry conference in a few months and they're hoping you've launched by then so they can drop a few lines about it on stage. They know the history of attempts to solve this problem, and they know lots of insiders who understand why they didn't work out.

The Lifeline

This is your friend. They're in the room for emotional support, while calling out your bullshit. They can appreciate how hard it is and, at the same time, giving you an honest perspective on where you could be doing better. It's great to have a friendly face in the room to make the whole thing less intimidating, or so you thought until the moment they started dropping truth bombs about how it's obvious that you and your co-founder need to split up because you're not bringing out the best in each other.

You can pay these folks in dollars, sometimes in pizza, and if your company becomes a real thing, they may want small chunks of equity (think 0.10%).

A lot founders don't really feel the need to have this kind of external accountability. It makes sense. To be a founder in the first place means having a strong sense of agency and belief in your ability to manifest something out of nothing without a lot of help.

Not only that, founders get a lot of warnings from other founders about "losing control" and to be careful about ceding too much power to investors and board members.

I'll let you in on a little secret on why you should welcome the help—from your pre-board when you first start out and from real board members as you bring on capital.

Investors don't actually like to do more work than necessary. Replacing a founding team is *a lot* of work. In an ideal world, we check in every now and then and the founder is completely on top of everything they're doing, shares enough reporting to indicate that, and is totally self-sufficient.

That's the founder we want you to be. That gives us more time to kitesurf, microdose, or tweet our misguided crypto libertarian leanings.

So trust me when I say we really only get up in your grill when we feel like it's in the best interest of the company, our investment, and you too.

That's why it's important to give others enough information to form an objective and complete picture of the business. We can't check your blind spots, offer advice, intros, or other kinds of assistance unless we actually know what's going on.

How to Run an Efficient, Thoughtful Meeting

Keep meetings short, rhythmic, and grounded in a single doc. Early on, bullets beat dashboards. Over time, sophistication grows.

Standing agenda (60–75 minutes):

1. **Hypotheses** (what we believe)
2. **Goals** (what we did to test them)
3. **Inputs & Effort** (how many outreaches, demos, prototypes)
4. **Outcomes** (measurable results)

5. **Learnings** (what surprised us)

6. **Decisions & Next Bets** (what we'll do before the next meeting)

7. **Asks** (intros, talent, specific feedback)

Use simple status flags early: green = **on track;** yellow = **in progress;** red = **blocked**. As you mature, split updates into **Marketing**, **Product**, and **Financials**.
Example:

- Hypothesis: SMBs will pre-order our widget.
- Goal: Pitch 100 via a vaporware deck.
- Inputs: 127 emails sent, 36 calls, 12 demos.
- Outcomes: 4 pre-orders, 3 asked for features X/Y.
- Learning: Pain is real, but price anchoring weak; feature Y is table stakes.
- Next Bets: Raise price test on 10 more, build Feature Y stub, recruit 5 reference customers.

Over time, you'll start building up more and more sophisticated ways of tracking and your reports will start to subdivide into functional areas like marketing, product development, and financials (when you have dedicated investor money or a limited pool of your own capital you've decided to invest).

When you actually start to get some angels or small funds invested in either an angel or pre-seed round, you might choose the most useful person from your pre-board to keep meeting with. It doesn't have to be an official board meeting and it can just be an "update meeting."

Remember, these meetings are *yours*. You can invite who you want to them. Investors might have ways they like to work and opinions on how to make sure they're productive, but you have the final say. Don't let an investor dominate your time by insisting you meet with them separately, causing you to duplicate all your effort.

Adding a couple of invested parties who do this on a full-time basis can be enormously helpful. For one, they have the bandwidth and network to actually be really helpful. Two, doing this for a living means they've seen a ton of patterns for success and failure and can help guide you to the ones that are relevant for your business. Typically in a pre-seed round, you'll find that one or two of your investors enjoy being active with their portfolio companies and can add the most value. Don't force an investor who isn't used to playing this role to meet up with you because it's not going to be a great use of either of your time.

Investors are generally interested in your success, but I also understand how the stress of scrutiny and the fear of having all these new people to answer to can be really overwhelming. It's totally natural for your instinct to tell you to be protective. You may get some counsel from lawyers and others to do the same thing—to create walls and distance. In my experience, that never works out—because along the way inevitable missteps start to spiral when left unchecked, or founders fall down rabbit holes they never should have gone down more then two steps in the first place.

Instead of protecting yourself *from your investors*—find a way *work with them*. Channel their knowledge and energy in a way that works for you. You want to create a productive, informed back-and-forth where you feel challenged but not attacked. They should feel like they have a space to opine and to be heard while you retain ultimate control over direction. That's where both sides get the most out of meeting.

Chapter 4

You Can't Handle the Truth

Being Rigorous and Honest with Yourself

When I tell you that you need to build out your network, you might be thinking, "I know lots of people who think my idea is awesome—and I have lots of connections to even larger networks beyond them."

Yet, go-to-market is still the number one reason startups fail. Founders assume their "big network" will convert into customers, but it rarely does—for two reasons.

BD DOA

People and companies with large audiences won't share your idea nearly as far and wide as you hope. Whether you try business development strategies to access an influencer's followers or Verizon's 500,000 small business customers, they're not going to hand them over to an unproven startup that might not handle the volume. Recommending you could backfire and create headaches for their network. It's highly unlikely that Zara is going to put your sizing tool on their website if it causes people to shop less because they're distracted by the onboarding. Most times, they won't even bother taking that risk—especially since the person who controls the design of the site is paid to drive revenue, not minimize returns.

That's someone else's job.

They also don't own their network's attention as much as you think they do. When Verizon says they have "access" to all these businesses customers, do you know what they actually have?

Do they have control and influence over customer purchases or just a "partners" website behind a buried link that no one goes to because everyone sets their phone and internet bills to autopay?

One of my portfolio companies once did a revenue share deal with a telecom company that suggested they had hundreds of thousands of customers.

Do you know how many customers it sent to them per month?

One.

Two in a good month.

Business development. That's what they call it when you're not specifically selling something, but instead trying to get a custom deal that somehow benefits both businesses. It's how Uber shows up as an option for directions in a mobile map app or how the default "share to" links in a creator app go to Instagram or TikTok. When they work, it can cement a leader as the all-out leader in a category or catapult a growing startup to the next level. Most of the time, if you're at a very early stage, it can be a huge time waster for a startup. You wind up meeting with folks whose job it is to take meetings and paint rosy pictures about what deals might look like in the future, but who don't really have mandate, budget, or staff behind making it happen.

All Clique, No Buy

The other issue with the big network you think you have access to is that your friends and closest professional connections aren't valid test customers. They're not objective and rarely fit perfectly within your actual target market.

But everyone's excited, right?

Here's a short primer on founder excitement during your startup journey—and the three times you'll feel nothing but joy:

1. The eureka moment when the idea first sparks.
2. The public launch of your idea when your network floods you with likes, comments, and congratulations.
3. The exit when you finally cash out.

Moments one and three are useful motivation.

Moment two? Dangerous.

It feels good, but it's misleading. Friends and family see their role as being supportive, not critical. Some of them are simply taking out "schmuck insurance"—being nice to you now on the off chance you do make it.

This way, they can say they supported you way back when.

All of this applause is great for your confidence but terrible for your product. Your job as a founder is to tell the difference between support and *validation*.

But My Mom Likes It

When I played Little League, my parents were at every game. They cheered. They encouraged me. But they never told me the truth: I sucked. No one fixed my swing, so I never got better. (Until, that is, I was put on the "B" team with a bunch of kids who had never even played before. I'll save the inspiration I got from that "why not me" moment for my next book.)

As a founder, you need clarity, improvement, and, only when you're on the right track should you even want anything that sniffs of validation.

Too many founders are clearly drinking the Kool-Aid of everyone in their immediate circle saying things like:

"What a great idea!"
"That's going to be so successful!"
"Everyone is going to want that!"
"That is a huge idea!"

It's not just newbies either. Recently, I heard two startup veterans raising $18 million for an idea. They were halfway there on the raise. When asked about market validation among their target customers—parents in this case—they responded with, "Every parent that I talk to is excited about this!"

Sound familiar?

Did they really expect some other dad at the jungle gym to make things awkward by saying, "I don't think that's a good idea. I certainly wouldn't pay for it."

Kind words can feel great early on—especially after you've made the difficult decision to put your own money into something, take on money from others, or quit your job. This is a vulnerable state and it's understandable to have fear that you've made a colossal mistake.

Chances are, you haven't—but your idea still needs a lot of work. Even if you have, wouldn't you want to find out as early as possible—when you still have lots of time to turn things around, to go back to your job, or return some of the money raised?

Here's what your friends and family are not necessarily saying to you, but what you should be seeking out:

"I would pay X dollars if it did Y thing . . ."
"I already use X thing for this and I'm perfectly happy with it."

Your friends and family are not your target customer. You need feedback from actual potential buyers.

What your closest connections could be doing, but may not be, is the following:

> *"I tried it and I'd love to sit down and talk with you and share my user feedback."*

That's when they think it needs work.

If it's amazing, they would say something like . . .

"I'd like to introduce you to an important contact of mine for investment or as a potential customer."

Otherwise, what you've done is just getting apathy instead of engagement—and that's not a path to success.

You might say, "Well, that's not what I asked them for." True—but when you're onto something, people often volunteer to help out of genuine enthusiasm.

Intros are critical, because figuring out who to approach isn't always obvious. The best founders find their way to relevant customers, to peers who've solved similar (but not competing) problems, or to investors known for expertise in that space.

Think of it this way: When you share your idea with those folks, they're making an *investment choice*—even if you don't ask.

It might not be an investment of money, but they're choosing to invest time or spend social capital.

Most people choose to invest nothing beyond a "Congrats!" on LinkedIn—and even then, not everyone bothers. That's the bare minimum.

The Best Kind of Feedback

Real signals come when people give their time—digging in, asking questions, offering feedback, or even hating on it! Time is scarce, so when someone spends it on your idea for better or worse, it means they care about it.

No one bothers to complain about something irrelevant to them. I complain about LinkedIn constantly because I use it daily and expect more from it. If no one cares enough to critique you, they're apathetic, and apathy kills startups.

This isn't just consumer-facing—it's the same with niche professional markets. If you shared your idea with your network and no one reached out to get a demo, that's a big issue. Maybe you don't know a critical mass of your target customers, but then I wonder how you even spotted the problem in the first place?

Engagement—positive or negative—is the first real test.

An even bigger signal comes when people invest their social capital by making introductions. Writing a check is one thing; putting their reputation on the line is another. If I lose money on you, that's between us. But if I introduce you to a trusted contact who then loses money, that damages my relationship with them. That's why intros are the ultimate validation—someone believes in you enough to risk their reputation.

Here's a guide to get more out of initial feedback and the types of questions you should get answers to.

You want to know:

1. Do I have a credible advantage to being the one building this?
2. Is this a big enough problem to work on?
3. Will customers want my solution?
4. If yes to all the above, have I figured out a way to convince investors in a clear and compelling way?

The most important piece of feedback that you *could* get at this stage, but might not be, answers the first question. Asking whether you have a credible advantage really boils down to, "Why you?"

I'm sure a lot of people believe in you, but almost none of them are being as objective as someone might be for, let's say, an actual job interview. If you were interviewing for the position of founder of your own company, would you get the job?

I'm sure your mom would hire you, but how about a team of venture capitalists who have never met you? That's essentially what's happening when someone judges you during a pitch—they're hiring you to be CEO of this potential new portfolio company of theirs.

You might've had the idea, sure—but are you the right person to pull it off? Are you uniquely positioned based on your past experience, network, technical skills, or obsessive knowledge of the space?

This isn't a question of whether you're smart or hardworking. This is a matter of whether you can imagine someone better equipped to do this.

Knowing whether you have a true advantage is a combination of awareness of your own strengths and weaknesses as well as understanding the particular challenges of that business model.

If you're selling into government or school districts, it pays to have done that kind of thing before given how tricky the hurdles are to getting contracts.

If you're building a deep tech company, it pays to have technical training and perhaps advanced degrees.

That's where talking to professional investors early can be helpful. They've seen examples of companies being built that are similar to yours. They can tell you objectively whether they see your background as the "perfect" fit for this particular challenge or just an okay fit.

Not long ago I was talking to a friend who successfully built and sold a company selling maintenance log software to engineers who work in big buildings. He recently had his first kid, and we were talking about an opening in the market for logging all of your kid's various firsts.

He and his former co-founder had built this kind of software before—that part would be easy. Cutting through the marketing all of the various products advertised to parents, however, would be incredibly hard. There are plenty of parents who have good ideas about what should be built, but knowing how to market them is really where the rubber meets the road in this particular space. Everyone wants to be the next big thing that every parent recommends, but I can barely keep up with the emails my daughter's school sends.

"Oh, they needed to bring apples this week?"

"Glad I made lunch. It's pizza day."

I know this because I've backed multiple companies in the early childhood space as a venture investor. (It doesn't take an expert to see that, though. Any parent could tell you about the choices for things they could buy for their kids are overwhelming.)

My friend had never run a direct-to-consumer marketing campaign, so while he was a successful entrepreneur, he wasn't the best entrepreneur for this particular product.

Ask the Right Questions

There's a science to how you ask for feedback. Too often, founders ask something along the lines of "What do you think?" when they should be testing a specific hypothesis—or asking questions that you know will have difficult to hear answers.

"Why aren't you buying this?"

"What's your concern?"

Imagine if the job of housekeeper had never been invented and you were the first to ever propose it. You might say to your friend, "Imagine having someone come and clean your house for you. What do you think?"

They might say, "Sounds great!" but what you don't realize, they assumed *you* were going to do it, for free.

"Oh, wait. It's a stranger? How do I trust them not to take anything? What if they're just weird and I don't like having them around? I'm paying for this? Why would I do that if I could do it for free myself?"

Suddenly, the support you got for the idea falls apart—but all is not lost! It's okay if your first few conversations are duds. That doesn't mean the idea is dead—it means you've started the process of learning. Great startups are often built after dozens of pivots and iterations, not out of the gate.

What you should be doing at this point is understanding what would get someone comfortable with a stranger coming to clean their house.

"What if I told you everyone was background checked?"

"What if you could see ratings from previous customers?"

"What if this was advertised as a deep cleaning service and they brought in a rug steamer, which is equipment you don't have?"

Other ways to run tests or measure interest beyond conversations include:

1. A landing page with a waitlist.

2. A cold outreach email to target customers.

3. A short survey to people who should care about the problem.

Then, you'd be getting right down to the heart of what resonates, what doesn't, and how much someone would be willing to pay—more useful information you're not getting from your supportive friends and family.

It's not their job to validate your startup (or invalidate it). It's yours to find out whether there's something real behind your idea—and you do that by getting out of your bubble and testing it with people who actually matter.

Back in 2007, I was one of the earlier users of Twitter—and one of the first to put it on the radar of venture capitalists. About a year after it launched, it was still very much under the radar, but a big percentage of its users went down to the SXSW conference in Austin. It was like a glimpse into the future getting to see what it would be like if everyone was on it. I told Fred Wilson of Union Square Ventures, who I had previously worked for, how it was taking off. That caused him to join the site two days later and fund it not long after.

What's incredible about that story—besides the fact that it got me into Nick Bilton's *Hatching Twitter* book about the birth of that company—was that it stayed under the radar for so long.

In fact, it took Twitter almost two years to get to a million users. Do you know how long it took ChatGPT to get to a million users?

Five days.

Why Hasn't This Been Solved?

What's different is how much more interconnected the startup ecosystem is. Almost every VC participates on social media in some way and every founder seems to subscribe to one of a handful of highly followed startup newsletters. (You can find mine at thisisgoingtobebig.com.) Almost every major city has a startup accelerator, coworking spaces and dedicated funds—and they're all talking to each other.

That's why when you pitch your startup, you can't blame an investor for thinking that if this is a problem worth solving, someone would have come along already.

Plus, your customers are currently solving it somehow—perhaps poorly.

After all, being an entrepreneur is cool and lots of people are out there looking for problems to solve.

Yet, I find that founders are dismissive of any solution but their own. They'll criticize competition for the smallest things, or they'll say the competition is missing something big—a lot of times after doing little more than clicking around a competitor's website.

Founders avoid studying competitors because it's demoralizing. It sucks to see someone out there who looks better funded, more polished, and farther along. If your emotional reaction is to retreat into denial or wishful thinking, you're just delaying pain—and making it worse later.

Real competitive research involves signing up for their product and go through onboarding—or having someone who could be a real customer do it and give you their feedback. It means analyzing customer reviews and Reddit threads. It means contacting former employees to get all the details on how well they're doing or not doing.

Even if it is true that you've figured something out that they haven't, once you launch, aren't they going to figure it out?

You think they're just gonna send you a muffin basket?

Or, worse, one of those god-awful fruit bouquets?

Will they be unable to catch up to you and the . . .

[checks notes]

. . . *$500,000* friends and family round that you're trying to raise.

Good luck with all that.

Founders need to assume their competition is smarter than them and Figure 4.1 is proof, courtesy of a 2×2 matrix.

I love a good matrix. It helps me with a lot of my risk analysis, because it plots out all the possible scenarios of doing X thing or not in different circumstances.

Maybe your competition has figured something out that you haven't—or maybe they're idiots. In your court, you could assume they're smart or assume they're stupid. In reality, they'll turn out to be one or the other.

	The competition is...	
You assume...	Smart.	Dumb.
They're smart.	Healthy Competition	You win.
They're dumb.	You lose.	You both stagnate.

Figure 4.1 Your Competition

If you assume they're smart, and it turns out they are, then you'll work hard to figure out what they know and soon make that same discovery—perhaps a customer insight or a technical difficulty—faster than you would have otherwise. Maybe that gives you time to catch up. Now you've got a chance.

If you assume they're smart, and it turns out they're a bunch of slack-jawed goobers, then you've only widened the distance between you and them. You know even more than you did about your customers and strategy, covered all the angles and you're really going to impress the hell out of investors with the added confidence that comes from doing your homework.

Nice!

Let's say you assume that they have no idea what they're doing, so you don't do any extra work. It turns out to be true. I guess you saved yourself some work—but that's work that could have gone into learning more about customers and building key relationships with them.

It's like not doing the reading and not having the teacher call on you. You may have saved the embarrassment, but you still missed out on the learning—learning that would have made you a better fundraiser.

Your answers to inquisitive investors are going to be worse—even though your product is, in fact, better than your competition. You'll come off as dismissive when asked about them.

An investor will sit there think, "It doesn't seem like *anyone* has figured anything out in this space . . . I think I'll move on until I get better answers about what this customer really wants."

Not great.

Now, for our final 2×2 box, you assume your competition is sitting around scratching their butts. Unfortunately, you're completely wrong. They've figured out that they've been focusing on the wrong customer, wrong value proposition, too high a price point, or all of the above.

You think they're a bunch of goons while you toil away making all the same mistakes they started out making before you discovered them. Now you're falling behind every day that you don't get this ship turned around.

Now you're royally screwed. What's worse, you look lazy too.

The point is, in today's hyperconnected startup world, ignorance isn't a moat. You can't hide behind the idea that "no one's thought of this" when the odds are someone has—and they've been at it longer than you.

The founders who win aren't the ones who pretend the competition doesn't exist. They're the ones who know their competitors inside out, respect their intelligence, and still find a way to outlearn, outmove, and out-execute them.

Because when investors hear you talk about the competition, they're not just learning about *them*—they're learning about *you*. If you sound like you've done the work, you come across as prepared, credible, and coachable.

If you sound dismissive or vague, you come across like someone who's going to get blindsided.

Strong and Wrong

One of the reasons founders dig in on bad ideas is because they've seriously overcommitted to them.

Here's a typical budget scenario for founders:

They have an idea, so they design a product at a high level. Then, they go through the legals of starting a company and raise some friends-and-family money around their great idea.

They use most of that money to pay someone to build a pretty complete version of it. Their hope is that the traction they get from having a polished version will carry them through to another round of financing.

What they don't plan for is all the feedback they get when they put their product out there—and how much of it they'll have to rebuild once it gets in just one person's hands.

Not to mention, *hundreds* of people.

Obviously, if the founder is technical, they can skip a lot of this spend on building and get a product to market with much less cost.

In both situations, founders rarely allow for enough budget to actually reach enough customers to get the traction they need—especially in a mature social media landscape. Things just don't go viral the same way they used to. Facebook, Instagram, YouTube, TikTok, etc., would rather have you pay them to get eyeballs than promote you for free.

At the same time, bigger media outlets would rather cover the next $10 billion funding round of OpenAI than the launch of some new two person and a prototype startup. Smaller outlets have been replaced by influencers who are also looking to get paid.

In the face of all these uphill battles, empty-pocket founders who burned all their cash building proudly share that, "They got all their initial customers without spending a dollar on marketing" like it was some kind of badge of honor.

Sorry, but marketing is actually a basic function of a company.

Your company isn't just the product. It's the whole thing—employees, go-to-market plans, conversion funnels, brand recognition, etc. Investors aren't just judging you on your ability to get a product built. They're scoring and trying to assess your ability to hire a team and spend wisely on marketing in order to make something that looks like an actual viable business.

Saying you punted on a critical part of company building—the going to market—because you spent all your money elsewhere isn't something to be proud of.

What you want to do instead is spend *as little as possible* proving out that you know what you're doing in as many areas of a startup as possible.

Years ago, there was a startup called Aardvark that eventually got sold to Google. It would connect to your social network and use chat to figure out the exact right person to ask a particular question to. If you wanted to find out the best Thai food in Detroit, it would scan all the people you knew and pose the right question to them, or friends of theirs. It found exactly the right Motown foodie to ask, as opposed to letting you just shout into the void of an unforgiving algorithm.

What struck me the most was how seamless the interaction was. It felt like a chat with a person long before AI was actually doing that well.

What I found out later was that the team hand built the product without code, doing every step manually and testing the results. You would type a question into a form, and the team would then go and scan through all the profiles of the people you knew in a regimented way to try to figure out who to send the question to—first just people who called themselves foodies, then just people who have ever lived in Detroit, then people who had Thai last names.

Each input would get tested and added or not added to the ending algorithm.

The first question took something like 38 hours to get answered. They kept plugging away, making manual adjustments and tweaks to language, searching for the right person, responses, etc., until they got it down to eight minutes.

That was before they wrote their first line of code.

They wasted no money upfront on expensive software engineers before creating a no-code solution and optimizing the hell out of it. It was the software equivalent of trying to sell your special muffin recipe at a street fair before signing a long-term lease for a bakery.

Overbuilding before you get customers involved isn't just a waste of money. It's a trap.

When you've spent months and tens of thousands of dollars or more building a shiny product, it's emotionally hard to admit you might've gone down the wrong path. But, if you start small, test early, and leave room for pivots, the search for the better idea becomes the plan.

This has all been made a lot easier thanks to no-code products like Bubble (bubble.io) and AI-driven "vibe coding" apps like Lovable (lovable.dev). These platforms allow nontechnical founders to make early versions of online applications.

This way, you're not trying to market your first idea as the best idea. You're on a journey to disprove it or improve it and the first version is just the first step to learning what the path to success looks like.

That's how you stay agile—and survive.

The Venture Vultures

As you build your idea and get early versions of it out to market, you're going to run into a ton of "startup experts."

It's a giant industry—from accelerators to product studios, courses to conferences, and, of course, TV pitch shows.

There have never been more people lining up to support founders . . .

. . . and make a buck off them.

At the top of the list of the absolute worst out there are the brokers—the people who charge you money to make investor intros and raise on your behalf. It sounds like a great deal—you pay them a bit of cash and then they take a cut of what they raise. The cash isn't nothing, maybe $25,000 or something, but won't it be worth it when they raise $1 million for you?

It won't be—because most of them fall short. How do I know? Because for 20 years I've been on the receiving end of their cold outreach. Broker after broker would pitch me deals at the wrong stage, outside of my geography, and in sectors that weren't relevant to me at all. They'd send emails asking if I "or someone on your team" wanted to take a look, which ignored the fact that I was a solo GP with no other team members.

In short, they had no idea who they were emailing.

They were just blasting the same cold lists that you could easily grab off of someone's link bait post on LinkedIn. Someone paid a worker on Upwork $50 for the emails of every VC in North America and now they're leveraging it for likes and comments.

Even if they did come through, they're not likely to raise from high-quality investors. That's because the best investors don't get their deal flow this way. It signals that you aren't in high-quality networks and you also can't figure out how to break into them.

Some founders say they can't raise money because they're "not connected to VCs." This is especially the case for underrepresented founders and those outside of the Bay Area and New York City.

I call BS.

I'm in a pretty unique position to see the fundraising process play out for a wide variety of founders, successfully and unsuccessfully.

And while I'm normally one of the only investors to call out sexism and racism in the venture world, I'll also spend an equal amount of time calling out the bad advice being given to underrepresented founders—advice that I believe holds them back and demotivates them before they even get started, and, ultimately, perpetuates inequity.

That's why I think we need to be critical and skeptical about the "lack of connection" drumbeat and examine what it's doing to the way founders raise.

VCs and other "experts" advise against cold pitches, presenting warm connections as a requirement—one that underrepresented founders or those from atypical startup geographies often can't meet.

Yet, I know of not a single VC who can say that they've *never* taken a meeting where someone emailed them cold.

The result is that many underrepresented founders who can't find their way to a warm intro assume they're shut out of the process, or, if they do get intros, find that they have to pay for them in some way—often in equity given to accelerators and advisors selling them connections.

It's the "waiting for an elevator" effect.

If you're on the ground floor and you see someone standing next to the elevator, seemingly frustrated with how long it's taking for the car to come down, you're likely to stand and wait, or give up and take the stairs.

It doesn't occur to you that this person never pushed the button and that the doors might open for you in short order. And, honestly, if I'm the person waiting, and someone else pushes the button, it's tempting to think that person is kind of obnoxious.

"Oh, did you think I was an idiot and don't know how an elevator works?"

That fear of being obnoxious hamstrings a lot of founders trying to network—and that's understandable in a world where non-straight/white guys get scrutinized more than others.

You have to get over that—because if you need the connections and don't have them, you just have to brute force them. You have to risk being pushy, because your competition is getting ahead by doing exactly that.

Building a huge company means knocking down barriers and inserting yourself onto the stage as an upstart. Waiving the white flag on being able to do this with the very first job you have to complete as a founder isn't a great look—especially the way investors put themselves out there these days.

So many investors write newsletters, post on LinkedIn, X, even TikTok. They show up on podcasts and in interviews on YouTube. They all leave comments open and often put their email addresses out there.

Even if they don't, most of them can be found at firstname at firm's domain dot com. If you can't figure out how to scan the web for their thoughts, comments, and strongly held opinions, and craft a thoughtful outreach that reflects your relevant opportunity, how are you ever going to build a billion-dollar business?

Plus, only registered broker-dealers can legally take a percentage of funds raised as compensation in the United States. Many of these operators are not licensed and so there's legal risk associated with paying someone to raise if you're not careful.

Beyond the fundraisers there are various flavors of advisors, consultants, and others who you probably shouldn't be paying attention to either. There are some amazing ones that are 100% worth it, but their numbers are smaller.

Consider supply and demand.

There are only so many startups that make it big—and of those there are only so many key, early employees who have insider experiences of hyper-growth and generational success. Most of the time, these folks go on to start new things, or become investors themselves because they have insane amounts of drive and ambition.

Rarely do they hang around to teach first timers who start out as industry outsiders. Maybe they'll do it as a one-off—doing a speaking gig at a conference or in an accelerator—but it's not something they'll dedicate themselves to.

Yet, the demand for knowledge from the ones who really made it is huge. There are new ideas and new founders created everyday so there's always a new customer to sell on "insider secrets." That's why startup podcasts seem to do so well. If you can get access to one of the founders who made it, there are thousands of founders who want to be just like them who are willing to listen and learn.

At least with a podcast, you can scale the knowledge sharing of a real expert.

When it comes to a variety of other less-scalable startup services—customized coaching, deck creation, fundraising strategy, capital introductions—there are far more startups needing the service than verifiable experts with genuine knowledge and networks to go around.

Enter the "venture vultures"—throngs of success-adjacent professionals with impressive sounding backgrounds available to help, for a fee, for equity, or both. Sometimes, they get aggregated into platforms like Intro where an intermediary has an incentive to add more and more advisors to the platform, diluting the quality of the knowledge being shared.

Ever hear the phrase, "Success has 1,000 fathers?"

There is no shortage of people who take credit for the growth of successful companies in various, vague ways. . .

"I led growth" = I wrote a couple of tweets and made a Notion doc that never got used.

"Ran product" = Filed three Jira tickets and gave strong opinions in Slack.

"Was the first marketing hire" = Technically true, but it was a contract role for three weeks and nothing shipped.

"Helped raise the seed" = Forwarded a warm intro and never got a reply.

"Responsible for our biggest partnership" = Took the call after the CEO already closed the deal.

It's really hard for founders to tell the difference between who has world-class talent and who stowed away in the cargo hold of a rocket ship with little to no impact on the mission.

The one thing you can say about all of them is that almost no one will tell you that you should stop working on what you're working on because it absolutely won't be successful unless something major changes.

Why?

Your continued effort, and hope, is their gravy train. These cheerleading vultures are too happy to contribute to the hustleporn narrative of "Get 100 no's before your first yes," and "Don't let VCs tell you that you won't be successful."

The more you keep hoping that the next investor is the one, the more they get paid.

Yet, statistically, failing is what most startups *should* do, as quickly as possible, so the founder can move onto better ideas.

Founders Are Saying . . .

Maybe you should surround yourself with other entrepreneurs, then? At least they're in the same boat and don't have the conflict of trying to sell you advising to get in the way. The only problem here is the wisdom of the crowds.

When it comes to founders, the crowds are, well . . . not that wise.

Anytime you go to a founder event, get into a founder Slack channel, read a founder newsletter, you have to realize that anyone who has an idea can call themselves a founder. It's a bit like putting on a cape and calling yourself a superhero.

I mean, Batman did it, and he didn't even have any powers. He just had billions of dollars and an aversion to therapy.

That's why you have to be careful when you hear things like, "Every founder I spoke to said that investor doesn't invest in X," or "Nobody I know was able to raise without a technical co-founder."

Given that most founders don't make it, if you accept "commonly held" wisdom from large groups of founders, statistically you're going to be taking advice from people who have failed or who will eventually.

The same is actually true for investors. Most venture capital investors haven't had a company get to IPO. Many don't even return capital to their investors—and angels are even worse. They do, however, know something about how to get a check, even if they're not that good at figuring out who should get it.

The average angel investor loses money over a lifetime of investing and is trading wealth for interestingness and entertainment more than they're getting more wealth out of it.

Here are some good rules of thumb when it comes to taking startup advice:

1. **Make sure the person giving advice has *directly* participated in the goal you're trying to accomplish.** Take pitch advice for your first round from investors who write lots of first checks into companies (as opposed to junior analysts at large growth funds). Take revenue growth advice from founders and sales and marketing leaders who have achieved the kind of revenue numbers and high growth you're looking to achieve. Make sure they've done it for the type of company you are (B2B, B2C, etc.). You won't always be able to do this perfectly, but you should be conscious about what kind of experience expects are basing their advice on. I once heard a founder say they didn't need fundraising advice because they were close to "one of the founding team members at PayPal."

   That sounds great until you examine this under a microscope. A "founding team member" or "founding employee" isn't the same thing as being a founder. They were just an early hire and probably didn't participate in the fundraising at all.

PayPal wasn't the original name of the company either. PayPal was the result of a merger of a company called Confinity that did security for mobile devices and X.com, which was a payments company. Someone who described themselves as a founding employee might have started at one of these two places, but they might have just been there for the merger and name change, making them a far later employee and much less relevant to an early stage startup.

On top of all this, we're talking about a company that started over 25 years ago—so whatever this person learned at the time is ancient technology history.

One comment I'll also make about "advisors" is that if you do actually make someone an official advisor to the company, it may create more questions than it answers. If you do find exactly the right person to advise the company—someone who knows the ins and outs of this space, why people buy what they do, who the players are, etc., the question is why aren't they investing.

Ideally they're a person who is good enough to have achieved some success in it—do they not have $5,000 to put into this company?

Why not?

If the smartest person you can find in a space isn't wealthy enough to write even that size of a check—then can *anyone* make any money in this space?

If they have the money and you're telling me that anyone who invests will make a ton of money—why don't they think so? After all, they know more about this area than I do as a generalist investor. What concern do they have that they're not sharing?

The advisor page in their deck might be impressive social proof to you, but to me it's a list of rich people who know enough not to invest.

2. **Good advisors don't make assumptions.** When someone says, "You should raise the most amount of money possible at all times," they might be ignoring your financial goals. What if you're not in something for the long term? Maybe you're just trying to get something launched so you can flip it in an acquisition. What if retaining board control is really important to you? What if you want to turn it cash-flow positive and run it forever as a lifestyle business? Instead of giving out cookie-cutter advice, a good advisor starts from whatever your goals and constraints are and works within them.

3. **Advice might cost money and what you're paying for should be clear.** There's a philosophy in some circles that it's some kind of a sin to charge startups for your work or advice, and that everyone should be taking equity. Unfortunately, most of this equity isn't going to be worth anything in the future. It's not realistic to expect everyone to work for equity.

Trying to get everything for free also undervalues your own time. Instead of commuting around trying to get a bunch of coffees with folks, taking one meeting at a time with dozens of different people, it would take a lot less time to just find and pay the one or two people with the exact knowledge you need for a few hours of their time and, most importantly, their attention. Payment gets you answers, deliverables, and focus—on your timeline, not theirs. If that sounds expensive, remember this: the most expensive thing in your startup isn't outside advice.

It's your own time.

Founder Time Is Money Too

Founders chronically undervalue their time. They treat it like a free commodity—when in reality, unless you're independently wealthy, every hour you work has a real cost. You've got rent or a mortgage. You have to eat. In New York City, even if you're living with nine roommates in a Bushwick warehouse, it's hard to get your monthly personal expenses below $2,500.

Some founders do the break-even math: they're on a "996" schedule—9 a.m. to 9 p.m., six days a week—about 72 hours per week, or roughly 312 hours per month. With $2,500 in expenses, that works out to about $8/hour to keep the lights on. And that's the trap—because when you see your own time as $8/hour, you'll take on every low-skill chore yourself. Need something done for $1,000? You think, "As long as I can figure it out in 125 hours, I'll 'save' money."

But that's survival math, not founder math. In the startup game, you're not being paid to keep busy—you're being paid (eventually) to create enterprise value fast enough that someone will fund you.

Here's the real calculation: say you have nine months of savings to get to a small pre-seed raise at a $6,000,000 pre-money valuation. You and a co-founder are both working "996" schedules.

Hours per founder over nine months: 2,808

Combined hours: 5,616

$6,000,000 ÷ 5,616 = ~$1,068/hour

If you're solo, double it—your hours are worth over $2,000 each.

Now ask yourself: Should someone worth $1,000–2,000/hour be taking out the trash, fiddling with a $20/hour admin task, or trying to hack together something you could outsource?

Every low-leverage hour is stolen from the work that could make your company worth millions—and your runway is ticking.

Chapter 5

There's No Crying in Baseball

Doing the Hard Work

"Do you want money?"

That's the world's simplest pitch.

The answer, assuming you're giving that pitch to an adult with at least a minimum level of intelligence, is always going to be:

*"F*ck yeah."*

If you're not hearing that phrase when you finish up with an investor, it means that whatever you said to them during the meeting, you never asked them if they wanted money.

At least, that's not how they understood it—and that, my friends, is a *you* problem.

Forget what you've heard about investor bias and preferences. Forget the nonsensical questions they asked in the meeting that made you think their dad owns the firm. Forget the makeup of their team, the schools they want to, or how they never built anything.

So what?

Are you going to pick up your marbles and go home?

Or, are you going to slay them with the kind of pitch that makes them say, "Jeez, this is the last thing I thought I'd ever invest in and you're the last people I'd ever thought I'd get into business with, but honestly, I can't think of a single reason why this wouldn't work."

Only one time in my 20-year career as an investor did I ever see a first-time founder run the table—getting a yes from every single professional investor who was pitched.

It was a female founder—a new mom with a baby at home. She had started a jewelry company whose social selling apparatus was powered by tech. In fact, the pitch was so good that it made Rob Hayes of First Round Capital, one of the lead investors in Uber, say, "I don't know anything about the jewelry business, but that woman is going to make us a lot of f*cking money."

That's the moment when I was convinced that *anyone* had the potential to have a pitch so good that it could convince any investor.

The keys to her unlikely winning pitch?

1. **Confidence that comes from experience.** This founder had worked within the jewelry business for years. She was hired to launch brands for bigger companies before—and so everything she said about the opportunity wasn't something she had researched when she decided to become an entrepreneur. She was already in the space and saw the opportunity from the inside.

2. **Incredible sales skills.** She paid her way through college selling CutCo knives. This was a person who had closed sales lots of times before. She knew how to look someone across the table and get them to fork over money. She wasn't "hoping" that an investor would give her money. She was confident that she was good enough to do it.

3. **She was comfortable with skepticism.** Remember that quote from Bane in *The Dark Knight*?

    "You think darkness is your ally? You merely adopted the dark. I was born in it, molded by it."

    This is how this founder treated someone who doubted what she was saying. She "thrived" when someone discounted her.

It fueled her determination to turn them from a no to a yes. She stepped up to the challenge.

4. **Meticulous preparation.** She knew how she was going to go to market. She knew everything about her budget plan. There wasn't a single question she couldn't answer quickly, succinctly, and confidently without getting lost in the details.

At no point did she worry about which investors might have been sexist or unwilling to back a consumer product. She didn't care about who wondered whether, as a mom, she'd be able to have enough time to focus on her company.

She approached fundraising as if the only one who could impact the outcome was herself—and that if she did as good as she could do, no one was going to be able to say no.

There's no point to thinking of it any other way.

What are you going to do if you think the investor as a bias against you? Call them out in the meeting? If the only point of the meeting is to get money from them, what do you think your chances will be if you call them out?

How good will you be if their bias is all you focus on?

Not only that, but if you feel like the outcome was mostly due to external factors, you'll never improve. You'll walk out thinking, "Those people were never going to back me anyway."

That might actually be true—but what is also true is that *something* in your pitch probably could have been better. If your focus is on them, you won't change a thing about your pitch or your business model before the next meeting.

That would be a wasted opportunity.

If you treat every meeting as yours to lose, if you do lose it, you'll work hard to figure out what you did wrong. Maybe it wouldn't have been enough to convince every investor, but getting better and better after every pitch is going to benefit you in the long term.

No Excuses

Mindset alone won't save you if the story your results tell is full of holes. Too many founders undermine themselves before they even get into the room—often with what they think are reasonable explanations for slow progress.

"Growth stalled because of seasonality."

"We couldn't test marketing because we didn't have the budget for it."

"We couldn't build all the features we wanted to because our developer had to take a full-time job."

Anytime I spoke to a founder and I heard a sentence like this, I knew it was an automatic pass because my expectations as a VC were ludicrously high, unrealistic, and unfair.

Startups aren't fair.

They're designed for the unreasonable optimist who sees the stack of disadvantages and finds a way to play anyway. Your competitors will have more money, more people, more runway. If you can't figure out how to create an advantage in those conditions, you're not playing the right game.

On top of that, you should have unfair expectations of yourself and your early progress as well.

I get to invest in a portfolio of dozens of companies while you're putting all your eggs in one single basket. You're forgoing salary during your prime earning years. You're working nights, weekends, hardly seeing your family or your friends.

Shouldn't more things be going right early on if this is going to work?

If your technical lead has to leave to take a full-time job, why aren't they recommending this to someone else? Why aren't they offering to stay on to mentor and advise some younger developers who don't have a mortgage and two kids—just to hold on to some of the equity you offered them?

For every excuse that I heard about the difficulty in finding technical talent, I heard five examples of technical people who were crashing on co-founder couches, building for equity in their nights and weekends just because they were so excited about the idea.

Not all of those ideas are good, but when talented people can't help but try to get involved, your chances of success are exponentially higher.

Another one I've referenced before is "We don't have a marketing budget."

Is it really a lack of paid ad spend that is causing your growth to flounder? If you were really such a product genius, how come you haven't figured out clever hacks to get users 1 through 10 to invite users 11 through 50 and so on and so on? People are so hyperconnected these days, why aren't people telling all of their friends about it?

Plus, if money was really the only key to success in your space, how fundable would this idea even be? The second I funded this company, some other bigger VC would fund a competitor with more dollars, and they would just win.

You have to have some other ingredient present and working early on, because that's the one I'm counting on you to succeed with even though you don't have as much money as your competition.

Founders sometimes think they're reasonably explaining a problem. Investors hear it as an admission of fragility.

When you say, "We couldn't build features because our developer left," I hear, "Our company can be derailed by one person's life change." When you say, "We couldn't grow without a budget," I hear, "We don't have a scrappy, repeatable path to growth."

Before you bring me that explanation, run this test on yourself first.

Ask:

- Would this still have stopped us if I'd been more creative? If you can name even one unconventional path you didn't try, then you quit too early.

- Did we try at least three workarounds before concluding it couldn't be done? The first "no" you hear—whether from a customer, a candidate, or the market—is rarely the last word.

- Did this challenge make my pitch stronger or weaker? A real founder turns obstacles into selling points: "We grew without a budget." "We shipped without a full-time dev." "We found traction even in the slow season."

If your honest answer to any of those is uncomfortable, that's good. It means you've found the point where you need to raise your own expectations—before I, or any other investor, raise them for you.

The question then becomes: What if this thing isn't quite working as you had hoped it did?

I'll tell you what won't fix it—venture capital dollars.

Fundraising doesn't fix absent demand—it just makes the failure more expensive.

Go back to basics and figure out if there's anything here worth saving.

Find the customers who passed and ask them why. Not why they didn't like it in a polite, high-level way, but the real reason it didn't stick for them. You might think it's price or timing, but it's often something deeper and fixable.

Look for signs of real commitment. Is anyone willing to pre-order, pay a deposit, or sign a letter of intent? Would a design partner spend hours with you shaping the product, not just take a call for "feedback"? Interest is free. Commitment costs something.

Test fixes without a budget. If your onboarding sucks, rewrite the flow in Google Docs or Figma and walk people through it manually. If marketing isn't working, try one high-effort, hand-to-hand growth tactic instead of blaming the ad spend.

If you can't get traction without a pile of new cash, odds are you can't get it with one either. Solve the core problem first, even if the solution is ugly, manual, or embarrassing. Investors will forgive rough edges—they won't forgive a company that dies without a life-support system of continuous streams of good money after bad.

How Good Is Good?

Level-setting in the startup world is difficult. You think your pitch is great, but you didn't see the one that investors saw in the meeting right before yours.

Most founders aim to be great at the things everyone sees: pitch decks, traction slides, a few happy customers. But the real bar? It's often higher—and shaped by people with massive, often invisible, advantages.

When I was in college, I wanted to be the top finance recruit. I had the GPA, the internship, I ran the finance club. But what I didn't know was that other students were managing real money in student-run investment funds.

Had I known that was even possible, I would've figured out how to raise alumni capital and start one. That would've set me apart.

Instead, I was doing a great job at the visible stuff—without realizing there was a whole other tier above it.

Years later, I saw the same thing play out when I was evaluating restaurant tech startups.

Everyone had a prototype and a few unpaid beta customers—small cafés and local joints that weren't scaling. Then I met Wiley Cerilli, former head of sales at Seamless.

He came in with 100 SMB customers ready to pay—credit cards in hand—for a product that wasn't even finished.

Why? Because he'd lived this world. He used to sit in pizzerias watching vendors sell, absorbing what worked and what didn't.

He already had the restaurant sales playbook in his head—and it showed. It would have been unfair to expect any other founder to clear that bar. But unfair or not, that's what a fundable outlier looks like.

I told my partners, "I just met the guy we're going to back in the local space."

Calibration is incredibly difficult if you're not on the inside of your industry—and not just in your industry, but on the innovative side of it, where venture investors back the newest companies. It's like being in a nebula where stars are born.

If you don't know where the bar actually is, you'll aim too low without even realizing it.

So ask yourself:

- What does extraordinary look like in your category?
- Who is being backed by the people you wish would back you?
- What are the unfair advantages of the people who are winning?
- If you don't have them—what can you build instead to compete?

In venture, you're not being judged against effort. You're being judged against outcomes.

The bar—fair or not—is set by whoever's already cleared it.

Don't just try to follow the existing playbook. Write the one that everyone else wants to follow after you. That's how you reset the bar—for yourself, and maybe for the whole market.

Hairless Ideas

You may find the fundraising process to be extremely distressing—but what can't be "distressed" is your company.

Some investors specialize in turnarounds. They buy troubled companies cheap, fix them up, and sell them later for a profit. That's distressed investing. There's an old line: "With all this fertilizer, there must be a pony in here somewhere." Sometimes there is—a cash-flow stream, a valuable asset, something worth salvaging.

But that's not venture.

Early-stage startups don't have enough built up to justify a rescue job. Investors want something that doesn't have "hair" on it.

What Counts as "Hair"?

Hair can take many forms, and some of it is subtle:

- **Legal knots:** unclear IP ownership, employee lawsuits, messy contracts.
- **Financial baggage:** high-interest debt, bad early investor deals that can't be unwound.
- **Team drama:** co-founders at war, revolving-door executives, absent key hires.
- **Customer red flags:** high churn, fake traction, one "whale" customer propping everything up.

The point is: investors expect chaos, not hair. Scrappy execution, duct-taped code, imperfect ops—that's normal. But legal fights, ownership disputes, or crippling debt are a different category.

Those are wounds, not scars.

Founders often assume their biggest "hair" issue is the cap table. They worry they've already given away too much ownership. In reality, that's one of the easier problems to solve—but only if the investor already wants to invest.

I've worked through messy cap tables before:

- **The biotech founder whose former employer claimed 90% of his idea.** I told him what minimum ownership I needed to see. If he could negotiate back to that number, I'd invest.
- **The divorced founder whose ex-husband owned 40% of her stock.** We structured a fix: converted an angel's common shares into preferred (so he kept upside protection without over-owning), and created a new option pool that rewarded her with fresh equity over time. That way, what she earned going forward was hers alone.

Both of those fixes took me an hour or two. Why? Because I believed in the companies. I wanted to invest.

Sometimes the "hair" isn't in the company—it's in how the founder shows up.

- Getting defensive when asked about numbers.
- Blaming others for past mistakes.
- Being vague or evasive when something clearly doesn't add up.
- Pretending everything is fine instead of owning a challenge.

Investors aren't just buying your business, they're buying your judgment. If you dodge, deflect, or minimize, you're signaling that problems won't get solved—they'll just get hidden.

That's hair too.

If an investor doesn't believe, they won't spend five minutes untangling your problems. No one's going to roll up their sleeves to fix your co-founder drama, settle lawsuits, or restructure toxic debt.

Would you buy a fixer-upper house? Maybe.

Would you buy one on a radioactive plot of land? Definitely not.

Chapter 6

Keep Your Friends Close

The Importance of Trust

Every founder raising money is, in one way or another, saying:

"This is going to work. Trust me."

And to be fair, many of them believe it—deep in their bones. They'll walk through walls to make it happen.

But most fail to turn that emotional conviction into investor trust.

The biggest reason is downshifting.

They trade in their deep-seated motivations for building this company for cookie-cutter slide templates, monotonous pitchspeak, and buzzwords like "disruption" and "democratization" that investors have heard lots of times before.

We trust humans, not pitch decks.

What do you want the investor to feel—and what lines, images, or stats are going to deliver that punch? Sure, the information is all there, but if you don't provoke an emotion from an investor, they're not going to be able to trust you.

Trust is a feeling, not a formula.

The Varying Levels of Trust

Neuroscience shows that even when we think we're being rational, our decisions are heavily influenced by emotion. Emotional resonance creates connection, which is the foundation of trust.

You don't trust a founder because they show you a well-crafted spreadsheet—you trust them because you believe they'll follow through, care, hustle, or never give up.

That's a feeling—not a calculation or a completed checklist.

Yet even when founders lean into the feelings and vibes, they fail to convince anyone their enthusiasm will translate into sound decisions.

Walking through walls isn't a strategy.

You can't brute-force your way to product-market fit. You can't hustle your way into distribution if you're aiming at the wrong customer. Startups aren't just about effort—they're about judgment.

That too is a surprisingly emotional conclusion, especially when a founder can't speak to having done this exact thing successfully before.

Operational trust—the question of whether you can build and execute—often comes down to a sense of resilience, that you won't flinch when your perfect plan goes sideways and that you won't stop until you find the right answer, instead of being stubborn, strong, and wrong.

Trust also relates to your market knowledge—do you really *know* the customer?

You can show market analysis, TAM (total addressable market) charts, or surveys, but what really sells this trust is your obsession with the problem, your empathy for the customer, your lived experience.

When they ask, "How can I trust that what this founder is telling me about the market is true?," they're more likely to trust you when it feels like the market chose you to solve this problem, not the other way around.

Another emotion that comes into play for an investor is fear—fear of looking like you made a dumb bet or that you'll lose a lot of money. That's where plausibility comes in. It helps you understand why this opportunity can even exist and why it hasn't been solved before—and why they're not going to look stupid backing you.

You don't have to have started a venture-backed company before (though it helps) but even just starting *anything* and getting it off the ground shows your ability to take ownership, get something off the ground, and navigate in the darkness of uncertainty.

That shows that you're not going to get tripped up by the basics.

A lot of execution trust comes from perceptions of the community you surround yourself with.

Do successful people vouch for you?

This is emotional by proxy. Other people's trust becomes your trust. Warm intros, testimonials, founder referrals—these create a halo effect.

Logic can't compete with someone smart and successful saying: "I'd back them again in a heartbeat" or "I'd write a check if I could."

Will lots of people line up to trial your product, introduce you to customers, or make introductions to talent? Would there be a lot of people lining up to work with you on this? Or, are you a one-person parade no one's following?

Everyone is going to come upon something they've never faced before. The best people can quickly reach out to someone who has already solved this challenge in order to figure out the best way to overcome it themselves—and they have access to those people for a variety of reasons. They're playing in the right sandboxes, are earlier to markets, so their relationships have been around longer.

Figure 6.1 shows a scale that reflects increasing levels of community trust—as judged by what others say about you. This represents the rising intensity and credibility of third-party validation. Levels 1–4 are excluded because, frankly, no one's cutting checks at that level.

11 – Legendary
"I'd quit my job to work with them. I'd bet my reputation on them."
Ride-or-die status. People want to be associated.

10 – Evangelized
"They're the real deal. One of the best I've worked with."
You're part of someone's highlight reel.

9 – Advocated For
"You need to talk to them. I'd invest again without hesitation."
People push others toward you. FOMO starts here.

8 – Trusted
"I'd vouch for them. If they're in, it's worth a look."
Actively opens doors. Credibility is transferable.

7 – Respected
"Smart. Gets stuff done. No drama."
Known as competent. Low-risk, high-functioning.

6 – Credible
"They're solid. I'd take their call."
Reputable. Worth a meeting. No one's raving.

5 – Tolerated
"Yeah, I know them. They're fine."
You exist. No red flags, but no real enthusiasm.

Figure 6.1 Community Trust Scale: What Others Say About You

This scale goes to 11, because that's one more than 10.

What do you imagine you'd have to do for people to score 10s and 11s?

Have you done these things?

If you haven't, someone else who is pitching for a different idea probably has. Their network is making the forceful, *emotional* plea for this investor to write a check.

If you're not getting yeses, perhaps you need to stop working on your pitch deck and go work on increasing the passion level of your biggest fans—especially ones who are potential customers.

Your Raise Started in High School

Have you started fundraising?

Even if you haven't sent a pitch deck out to anyone yet, you have.

One of the biggest misconceptions in this business is that fundraising starts when you finish your deck and start the wave of VC and angel emails. The truth is you started your fundraising 10 years ago, whether you realized it or not.

That's what people don't get. They think fundraising is about proving out a business model or showing traction metrics and a polished pitch deck. And sure, that's part of it. But it's a tiny part—especially at the early stage. The much bigger lever is whether you've been the kind of person people wanted to bet on all along.

Did you build credibility when no one was looking? Did you consistently show up, help others, and earn a reputation that compounds over time?

If you're not sure where you stand with your network, test it. Go to the most successful or financially well-off people you know. Ask them if they have or would ever consider putting money into a startup idea that came from a trusted referral.

If they say yes, then ask, how much do you think you'd invest if the idea just blew you away—like you totally understand why it was valuable, it was in a space you knew, and it sounded amazing.

Then ask, "What if I told you I was starting a company, it was in a space I knew well, but we hadn't nailed down the idea yet? What would be my "blank check" number from you if a round was coming together?"

The spread between that number and how much more they'd invest if they already vetted the idea is an indication of how much more work you need to do to create "blank check" trust in your network.

If it turns out they'd invest *more* in a foggy idea that you were putting together versus a good idea where they knew the person less, congratulations. That's a real testament to your ability to build trusted relationships.

Early-stage investing is fundamentally an act of trust. Most investors have to make bets on markets they don't fully understand, products that will almost certainly pivot, and founders with little or no traction to show. There are too many unknowns to diligence your way into certainty. You can only get comfortable with the person sitting across the table—the way they think, how they handle setbacks, whether they'll keep showing up when it gets hard.

Fundraising isn't a transactional moment. It's the cumulative weight of every interaction you've had—every time you helped someone without expecting something back, every time you followed through, every time you demonstrated you could figure things out before you had any leverage to ask people to trust you.

My friend Ali Hamed, who has raised billions in investor capital, once told me: "People started raising money their freshman year in high school."

You don't get to show up one day and expect anyone to believe you can build a company from zero if you haven't spent years demonstrating you're the kind of person who can. There's no hack for that. You can't compress a decade of trust into a three-month fundraising process—unless you launched before raising and suddenly you have a 100,000 daily active users.

It's easy to forget this when you're early in your career, staring at other founders' headlines and thinking they must have just knocked on the right door or said the right thing. But almost every successful fundraise has years of invisible work behind it. The references who pick up the phone and vouch for you. The colleagues who say, "They've always been the hardest-working person I know."

The early investors who watched you operate and decided you were someone worth backing even when the product was half-baked.

You can't fake that, and you can't rush it.

If you're thinking about raising capital, ask yourself what you've been doing for the last decade to earn that privilege. Have you been building a reputation that compounds? Have you been making deposits in the trust bank so that, when the day comes, you're not cold-calling people to convince them you're worth a bet?

Here are the types of things you need to be doing:

Be visibly reliable in any context. People remember who does what they say they will do—every time. Show up prepared. Meet deadlines. Follow through. Even in your day job or volunteer roles, you're demonstrating whether you're someone worth betting on.

Help others without expecting immediate returns. Share advice. Make introductions. Offer feedback. Investors and peers notice who contributes to the ecosystem simply because they care. The founders who help without asking, ironically, get helped the most when it matters.

Build a track record of learning fast. Show you can step into an unfamiliar problem space, figure it out, and make progress. If you can demonstrate that pattern—at work, in side projects, in community efforts—people trust you'll adapt when your startup inevitably pivots. This is why a lot of founders come out of McKinsey or similar consulting companies—because all they do day in and day out is parachute in and learn.

It helps that a lot of the network that you build in those types of companies has a lot of money to invest as well.

Develop a reputation for transparency. Investors don't expect perfection—they expect honesty. Be the person who's upfront when something isn't working, who shares both wins and losses. Over time, that signals you can be trusted with someone's money because you won't sugarcoat bad news.

Be consistent over time. Trust compounds. If you're only visible or helpful when you want something, people sense it. Keep showing up for your community, your network, and your peers year after year.

Become known for something. Whether it's a domain (e.g., marketplaces), a skill set (e.g., growth), or an approach (e.g., product storytelling), be the person people think of first when that topic comes up. It's easier to trust someone who clearly knows their lane.

Stay in touch and stay top of mind. The founders who get blank checks aren't the ones who go dark for five years. They're the ones who regularly check in, share what they're learning, and make people feel connected to their journey.

Treat small asks like big ones. If someone gives you their time, their advice, or a tiny early intro—treat it like they handed you $1,000,000. Gratitude and follow-up are memorable.

Create positive social proof. When people hear from multiple sources that you're smart, dependable, and good to work with, it creates a three-dimensional picture of credibility. Even a small group of well-respected supporters can be the difference between "Who are you?" and "I've heard great things."

Because the truth is, when you walk into that first pitch meeting, you're not starting at zero. You're starting wherever you left off in all those tiny moments years ago when you could have opted to do the easier thing or the transactional thing or nothing at all—and you didn't.

So if you're reading this and you haven't started yet, consider this your reminder. The best time to build your fundraising foundation was 10 years ago.

The second-best time is today.

Chapter 7
To Infinity... and Beyond! Going Big

Answering "How much are you raising?" feels a bit like bidding on *The Price is Right*:

- Bid too low and you'll lose out to a more aggressive founder whose ambition signals a strong chance at a big exit.
- Bid too high and you'll lose because you have unrealistic expectations and seem a little bit naive—or you've got an inflated sense of what you've built.

No need to get too stressed over it, because this isn't the right way to look at it anyway. If a founder walks into a VC trying to guess what the "right number" is, they're looking for the right answer on the wrong side of the table.

The founder should be the one choosing a number and making their strongest case for it. The number should be built on future milestones, not prior accomplishments. Remember, we're selling tickets to the future, not rewarding someone for what they've done up until this point.

You should be budgeting your raise to get to the next obvious step—the step that de-risks the *next* raise as significantly as possible. This isn't just a function of time. It's all about accomplishment.

Once I asked a founder what this round would get them. They responded, "This would be about 18 months."

I'm quite sure they could *spend the money* in 18 months. Who couldn't? What I cared about was once that time at passed, what does the money buy you, besides time? What milestones will we hit? Is it a company I'd be a happy equity holder in 18 months from now?

Certainly not if all they did was spend the money with no results!

Goooooooooooals!

In the beginning, you might raise to get to a product if you don't have one yet. Having a product versus not having one is obviously a huge difference.

The next goal after that might be proving out consistent growth by finding product-market fit or maybe early monetization. Honestly, that all depends on what kind of product you're building.

This is also why surrounding yourself with people who have done this before—being in the flow of best practices and what's "typical"—is so incredibly important. If you're trying to start a tech business in Oklahoma and you don't know anyone who has ever raised venture or sold a venture-backed business, and you've not actively conversing with any investors, I have no idea how you'd figure out what the right milestones are. You wouldn't know, in the current market, whether what you see as milestones would be "enough" for an investor to see it the same way.

You *could* listen to VC-backed founders and VCs on podcasts, read their newsletters, etc., but that wouldn't get you tailored feedback to *your* specific story.

For example, if you were building some B2B SaaS software, getting usage is nice, but proving out willingness to pay and how much is really the big step.

Whereas if you were building a dating app, where there's lots of proven willingness to pay, but few sites that capture virality and get to product-market fit, hitting viral coefficients and high growth would be more relevant milestones.

Whatever your story, you're ideally going for the milestones that make the next check an obvious and undeniable yes. We're not just taking break even. We're talking about being able to write an investor intro email that converts into you being the hottest fundraise in the market.

Why aim for anything less?

What Your Ask Says About You

Remember that your ask sends a signal about:

- Confidence *and* ambition ("Do you believe this is venture-scale?")
- Market awareness ("Do you know how rounds are typically sized in this space?")
- Competence ("Do you understand how to budget for milestones?")

Founders don't always realize that VCs aren't just evaluating the math of the plan—they're reading the ask itself as a data point.

I remember a founder who was pitching $400,000. When I asked her why so little, she gave me the following:

"I'm a female founder."

"I don't have a technical co-founder."

"I don't have enough traction."

I said, "If I wrote you a million dollar check right now, would you not know what to do with it?"

"Of course I'd know what to do with it," she responded confidently.

She proceeded to list out a bullet point plan of two critical hires, faster go-to-market movement, and several other strategic moves that were a much more compelling pitch than just trying to break even on the $400,000.

This is the difference between two types of budgeting:

- **Operational budgeting** = "What do I need to keep the lights on?"
- **Strategic budgeting** = "What gets me to undeniable next-round proof?"

The great founders budget like strategists, not accountants. You can think like an accountant when we're talking about how little we have left when we're trying to cut the budget during hard times.

Like most founders, she didn't want to spend all her time fundraising. Besides the assumption that raising more was harder, she just wanted to get back to work.

I convinced her to raise a bit more—at least $750,000, but perhaps up to $1.5 million and got her to agree to a 2–3 week sprint. I reached out to about 15–20 other investors. Half were interested in taking a meeting and multiple funds committed.

She wound up with over $2.5 million of interest—and that's not even counting the investors who indicated interest that we unfortunately had to ghost because the round quickly filled up.

The pitch for more money was a definitively better pitch. It also took far less time to raise her round than she would have spent nickel-and-diming this for small dollars—but asking for more money runs counterintuitive to how struggling founders think.

Her small ask was playing right into the very bias held by investors—that women aren't aggressive enough. If you're socialized to believe that women are far less likely to take big risks and aggressively build something big, then a female founder who comes in asking for $400,000 to get to break even is going to look like an unlikely candidate to return your fund.

I don't think in all my 20 years of venture capital investing I ever had a straight white male founder come in and ask me for less than $1 million. Perhaps the only exception to that would be a couple of hacker types who just need enough to quit their jobs or put contract work aside to see if they could get a prototype of something that could be big to work.

The real danger isn't asking for too much—it's asking for too little.

Once you model what it takes (people, product, marketing) to get to your big next goal, leave some cushion to actually fundraise again once you get there. A good fundraising cushion is usually about six months, making each raise *typically* last around 18–24 months. For most companies, that's just what it takes to iterate through multiple product/customer experiments after you've built something.

The Ownership Question

A lot of founders worry about the price of a round. If you raise more, won't you have to give up more of the company?

Yes, but you're decreasing the chance that you run out of money. Would you rather own less of something that had enough money to get to all its milestones or 100% of something that ran out of cash?

I'm sure you feel like you won't run out. You've re-run the numbers on your financial model nine times over.

Let me tell you: shit happens.

An angel investor once told me that things either cost twice as much as you think and take three times as long or cost three times as much and only take twice as long. The only problem is, you don't know which.

This is further supported by the fact that I've yet to meet a founder who sold their company for at least $100 million whose main regret was taking too much capital in their first round of financing.

They have no regrets because they had enough money to make it through all the ups and downs.

Meanwhile, I could throw a huge party with all the founders I know who wished they had just a few hundred grand more in the bank at the right time.

I know you don't want to raise too much. I know you've read the horror story LinkedIn posts of the founders who sold their companies for hundreds of millions but the VCs took all of it, leaving the people who started it and their employees with nothing.

Those stories never tell the whole story.

If you take $300 million of other people's money to build a company, and after spending all that money, you only built a company worth $300 million, should you really make a profit when it gets sold?

After all, having raised that much, you were probably making a nice salary the whole time.

You have to create more value than you take in funding. That seems pretty fair to me.

Founders often think about dilution in the wrong way. They picture it like subtraction: "I sold 20% last round, I'll sell another 20% this round, and soon I'll have nothing left." That mental math makes dilution feel scarier than it really is.

Dilution isn't subtractive. Each time you raise, you're selling a percentage of what you still own—not of the original 100%. If you own 80% after your first round and then sell another 20%, you're not giving up 20% of the whole company—you're giving up 20% of your 80%. That leaves you with 64%. Do it again, and you're just over 50%. After four rounds of ~25% dilution each, you'd still own about a third of the business, not some tiny sliver.

The takeaway: you don't "bleed out" to zero just because you raise multiple times. Yes, you'll own less over time, but the slices get smaller each round, and as long as the company keeps growing, you're still left with a meaningful—and hopefully much more valuable—piece of the pie each time.

The Secret to Owning More

If you're really trying to optimize for how much you own at the end, raise less often instead of worrying about the price each time.

The decision to raise again accounts for the bulk of dilution; the exact price you negotiate only shifts your ending ownership by a few percentage points. Shaving off 5% here or there isn't nearly as impactful as being able to grow the company far enough that you can skip a round entirely.

The big picture: if you can keep building toward the next obvious milestone without going back to market, you protect your ownership far more than you do by haggling over valuation point spreads.

Don't believe me? Build yourself a model.

Imagine you sold 23% of the company in each of five rounds. After five rounds, you'd own 35% of the company:

$$\left[\begin{array}{c} 100\% \times (1-23\%) \times (1-23\%) \times (1-23\%) \\ \times (1-23\%) \times (1-23\%) \end{array} \right] = 35.1\%$$

Sell this thing for a billion dollars and you've got $350 million (before taxes, obviously).

What if the pricing of each round was much worse and the VC's wanted 7% more every single time, taking a total or 30% with every financing?

You'd still own 24%

$$\left[\begin{array}{c} 100\% \times (1-30\%) \times (1-30\%) \times (1-30\%) \\ \times (1-30\%) \times (1-30\%) \end{array} \right] = 24.1\%$$

Less, yes... but a billion-dollar sale still nets you over $240 million.

Now let's say that after the first three rounds, you decide to move toward profitability. Sure, you grow more slowly and take longer to get there, but you own more at the end. Plus, your risk goes down because you're not subject to the fundraising markets. A VC nuclear winter wouldn't harm you because you're profitable.

What's your ownership then?

$$[100\% \times (1-30\%) \times (1-30\%) \times (1-30\%)] = 34\%$$

Put another way, you'd own enough that you'd only have to sell the company for $700 to make the same amount as you did when you took five rounds, going back to the market two more times and risking the whole company's survival on VCs saying yes each time.

In the beginning, you probably can't bootstrap. Even if you can, you're probably going to move too slow if you're really gunning for a big exit in a fast-moving category with competition all around you. Once you break out, however, you have a lot more flexibility on how you run the company and when you take money.

Just because you got on the venture train to start the company doesn't mean you have to continue on it forever. Make those choices when growth and solid market position have been de-risked if you're really concerned about ownership.

You may have heard the term "seedstrapping." That's when you raise just enough to get to profitability and then you grow from there in a self-sustaining fashion. It's an interesting strategy, because it also lowers the bar for what kind of exit your investors will find interesting, given that they're not seeing their ownership get diluted either. You might not build the next IPO (initial public offering) this way, but only raising one round takes maintaining ownership to the extreme, while acknowledging that not everyone can bootstrap from the beginning.

Regardless of which strategy you choose—to raise as much as it takes (and more) or to focus on getting to profitability, the math will always say don't sweat the price too much.

Obviously, you don't want to get fleeced, but if you do your best pitch and talk to enough people, you'll get a market price. Whatever people want to pay at the time that you're selling is the price your company is worth.

Just don't let that article that Carta published on the average price of seed rounds fool you. Sure, you want a fair market deal, but what they're not publishing is how those numbers got where they were.

These surveys only publish the value of *equity* rounds once they close, not SAFEs or convertible notes. While these lightweight mechanisms may have a price cap, they don't technically have a price. That means that any pricing information you see is from companies successful enough to make it to a priced round—a curated selection of early winners.

And the size of those rounds?

That takes into consideration all of the previous capital raised through various instruments that converted into the new equity.

That $8 million seed round priced at a valuation of $25 million?

That was actually $500,000 friends and family done on a SAFE with a cap of $3 million, another $2 million pre-seed done on a cap of $8 million, and then a $1.5 million extension done at a $12 million cap.

It was only $4 million of new money—raised after the company spent $4 million getting to some really terrific milestones that *almost* put it in contention for a Series A.

Don't believe the hype.

Fast Doesn't Have to Mean Stupid

Another reason that it's sometimes hard to get founders to raise more is because they feel like moving too fast is reckless. Companies that raise lots of money and hire tons of people fast make big news when they fail—while no one says a word about the death of companies run by cautious founders that bled out slowly.

Waiting for perfect information? That's like running out the clock when you're behind by three touchdowns. If you're cash-flow negative, you're burning money every single day you don't grow.

Slowness doesn't protect you. It quietly drains the lifeblood of your company—cash.

The most dangerous part? It doesn't even feel like risk. It feels like prudence. It feels like discipline.

But it's not.

It's hesitation disguised as strategy.

The Psychology of Caution

Most founders don't sit on their hands because they lack ideas. They sit on their hands because they don't fully trust their ability to execute. They assume things won't work out, so they want certainty before committing.

They also don't trust their ability to raise. They may have felt like they got away with one the first time around, maybe because they told a good story. They know that the stakes will be higher next time and that they need to execute.

Executing, however, doesn't mean not making mistakes. You can make all the mistakes you want as long as they don't cost you too much in time and money—and the way to prevent this is to pull back from mistakes quickly before your overly cautious nature and fear of looking rash or incompetent lets them fester.

The kind of hesitation that sinks a company shows up in three ways:

The flinch reflex. You make one bad hire or miss one target, and suddenly you want proof before doing anything again.

But startups don't offer proof. They offer bets with odds. Waiting until you're "sure" is waiting forever.
- **Fear of being wasteful.** Holding cash feels responsible. You tell yourself you're "protecting runway." But if you're not putting that money to work, you're not extending life—you're just stretching out the countdown clock to the same ending.
- **The false idol of optionality.** Keeping options open feels powerful, but optionality is useless without motion. Money in the bank with no growth plan is like keeping the car in neutral while the gas runs out.

This is where cautious founders get trapped. They mistake hesitation for discipline. But discipline isn't about waiting—it's about knowing what to do next and doing it with focus.

Believing in your ability to execute isn't arrogance. It's survival.

Execution Earns Belief

Confidence doesn't show up in the mail. You earn it by doing the thing—and then doing it again. If your first salesperson closes deals, the belief isn't "maybe they got lucky." The belief is: I can recruit, train, and manage someone who sells. At least, it *should* give you that sense.

That's the process worth betting on.

If you ship a feature and customers adopt it, don't write it off as chance. Believe in your ability to run discovery, prioritize the right problem, and execute a build.

That's what's repeatable.

If one investor meeting sparks interest, don't tell yourself it's a fluke. It means your story connects. The belief is that you can keep refining it and repeat it at scale.

Momentum doesn't come from waiting until you know for sure. It comes from stacking proofs of execution and trusting the process you've built. You don't need perfect foresight. You need confidence that you can keep solving the next problem.

The Math of Speed

Here's the math: when you're burning money, time is your enemy. Every week you hesitate, your runway gets shorter and your numbers look flatter. That makes the next raise harder.

If you wait three months to hire the second salesperson after the first one succeeds, you've lost three months of compounding revenue. That revenue is gone forever.

If you wait to launch until every bug is ironed out, you've lost months of customer feedback—and burned cash producing polish nobody asked for.

If you wait to scale marketing until you're "ready," your cohort growth stalls. That flat line will be staring you in the face during your Series A pitch.

This isn't theoretical. It's arithmetic. Time compounds against you when you move slow. Time compounds for you when you act on what you've learned.

Reframing Risk

The irony is that moving fast feels risky, but moving slow is risky. I get it. Fast risk is visible. If you hire too soon, the failure is obvious. If you launch too early, the flaws are public. If you scale too quickly, you might stumble.

Slow risk is invisible. Your burn quietly eats runway. Your growth numbers sag. Your next round becomes impossible—not because you blew up, but because you never took off.

Which risk would you rather own? The visible mistake you can learn from and correct, or the invisible decay that kills you slowly? How long do you think your best talent will stick around if they signed up for a high-flying startup and you haven't hired anyone new in four months?

Founders tell themselves that going slow keeps them in control. But the truth is the opposite. Slow founders let time and burn dictate the outcome. Fast founders—when they move with conviction—bend time back in their favor.

Conviction, Earned in Advance

Speed should be a result of conviction and conviction should come from preparation.

When you've:

- Hired people who know how to deliver,
- Mapped the economics of your model, and
- Studied the market enough to know what's possible . . .

. . . you've earned the right to move quickly. Trust yourself when things start to work.

To Model or Not to Model

The two best ways I know of starting a heated argument are talking politics on Thanksgiving and opining on the value of financial models to early-stage founders.

For every expert who has ever said that "projections are bullshit," there's another who says that building a model is the core to understanding your business.

Who's right?

Financial models are going to be 100% wrong *and* building one is still an incredibly valuable exercise. You don't need to be a Wall Street banker to model your business either. You need just enough to know where the ramps and cliffs are.

Here's what every good first financial model should help you answer:

- How long will the money last?
- What milestones is it *possible* to hit before you run out of cash? (Not *probable*. We want to know what this could do if it works and everything went the way you hoped it would.)
- What drives revenue? (Please don't say the hardcoded row of monthly percentage growth that you pulled out of thin air.)
- How much does it cost to serve one customer? (This is what we mean by "unit economics.")
- What does it take to acquire a customer?
- Who do you need to hire and when?

Bonus:

- What breaks if you go faster?

A financial model helps you figure out what's *possible*. There's a point at which you can tilt the hockey stick so high that even you don't believe it. Keeping within the limits of plausibility helps you and your potential investors understand whether all of this effort is going to be worth it.

It also keeps you honest about whether you've done enough research. When someone says, "Where did you get this cost to manufacture number from?" or "How do you know you'll be able to acquire this many customers with this marketing budget?," you better have an answer that's anchored in reality.

Great answer: "I got four quotes from manufacturers who would give us this cost for our first product manufacturing run—and they also told me how low they can go at high volumes."

Not so great answer: "A 90% margin seemed like too much and 50% seemed too little—and I know VCs like at least 80%, so I picked 82%."

Building out a financial model also forces you to consider all the inputs and assumptions that go into driving revenue. It's a basic cause and effect model:

I do some things and money appears.

Those things might be hiring engineers to build a product, a marketer to create awareness (provided they have a budget to work with), and some salespeople to close the deal. Most of your costs early on are going to be people if you're building something online, plus materials if you're building a physical product.

The great thing is that every single number you put in is an assumption that can be tested, because there's ultimately a person responsible for driving each one.

How much can a marketer grow your business? Ask a prospective marketer with experience something along the lines of, "If I gave you this budget for this product and held you to these top-of-funnel goals for our email list and socials, could you hit them?"

Salespeople will have quotas driving most of their comp, so they'll tell you what's realistic.

Technology leaders will tell you the size of the team they'll need to build out the product as you've laid it out, and what salaries they'd likely have to offer.

Most people aren't going to want to take a job they'd fail at, so you can test your model while building out your talent pipeline at the same time. Talking to potential employees is something you should be doing as early as possible to both build a funnel and see how realistic your goals are. If you do raise money, you'll have to hit the ground running with your hires, so this won't be a wasted effort.

Obviously, you can start simple and get more complex and detailed as you move forward. Putting enough numbers down just to understand how long it might be until you break even or how much you might need to sell is a good start. Then you can start to lean in and understand what the limiting factors are for growth—and the drivers.

Financial models are also great for early teams and co-founders to get on the same page. They're a shared vision of the operations of the company in the early days, so when you put everything down on paper, you lower the chances of miscommunication and missed expectations. There's no chance that your co-founder starts pushing for international expansion in your second month when your financial plan clearly outlines your first European sales hires in year three.

They're also a way for investors to test your thoughtfulness and insight—as well as your coachability.

If an investor thought your assumptions weren't aggressive enough, they might ask, "Why not double the pace of new location openings?"

A bad answer would be, "That would feel too fast."

Why?

Are we running this company on vibes or real data? They want to know where it would actually break.

A better answer would be, "It's taken me at least four months to scout a great location for a new store opening. If I had to do that every two months instead of four, that would cut into my other responsibilities. Either I'd have to drop marketing or I'd have to hire a head of real estate to do scouting full time. Either way, that's going to add about $150,000 to the budget, which would cause us to run out of money before our inflection point—and I wouldn't want to have to fundraise before that."

That's a great answer because it shows that you know the ins and outs of how this business works and what drives it. It also shows that you have realistic assumptions about the limitations of all the individuals involved, and what kinds of hires you'd need to support them when more work needs to be done.

This might drive an investor to say, "Well, I think growing more aggressively improves your chances of a next round, so what if I gave you an extra $500,000 to hire that expansion person *and* the marketing person to make sure the locations get traffic? Wouldn't the pitch for the next round look better based on the results those people could drive?"

At that point, this investor is already imagining themselves investing in the company and telling you how it's all going to play out. Your vision has become theirs and they're mentally and emotionally in too deep not to invest, which was only possible sitting around a financial model playing with the numbers.

So how do you make this happen?

How to Build a Stage-Based Financial Model

First off, forget the idea that you can map your business month by month like a corporate budget in a defined timeframe with each month assuming you're basically running under the same rules for 18 straight months.

Early on, what matters isn't the exact slope of the curve, but whether you can cross the right milestones. A good model shows the sequence of stages and what it costs to move from one to the next.

Stage 1: Build and Test

Goal: Get a working product into the world.

> **Inputs:** Engineering and design salaries, contractors, tools, maybe regulatory costs.
> **Outputs:** A real MVP in the hands of real users.

How to model it:

- List who you need to hire (or contract) to get version 1 live.
- Estimate their costs and the time range (e.g., 3–6 months).
- Your model answers: What's the minimum cash to get to something people can touch?

Stage 2: Founder-Driven Sales/Limited Go to Market (GTM)

Goal: Prove people will pay.

> **Inputs:** Founder time, maybe one sales hire or a marketing experiment, small tools budget.
>
> **Outputs:** Actual customers, not just signups or LOIs (letters of intent).

How to model it:

- Assume you are the main salesperson at first. Add only minimal GTM spend.
- Put in a range: "6–12 months to land 10 paying customers."
- Your model answers: How much does it cost to validate product-market fit (PMF), and how long might that take?

Stage 3: Gas on the Fire (Post-PMF)

Goal: Scale what's working.

> **Inputs:** Dedicated sales team, marketing budget, more engineers to handle growth.
>
> **Outputs:** Consistent revenue growth and improving unit economics.

How to model it:

- Start layering in headcount for sales, marketing, and product.
- Add spend that accelerates customer acquisition (ads, partnerships, expansion).
- Create scenarios: What happens if you grow 2× faster or 30% slower?

Your model answers: What would it take to scale, and what breaks if we go faster than planned?

Why Stage-Based Models Work

They flex. Instead of pretending you know whether it'll take 9 months or 18, you show investors the milestone that defines success and the range of costs/timelines to get there.

They de-risk. Each stage has a proof point: MVP (minimum viable product) built, paying customers, repeatable growth. That's what makes fundraising easier at the next round.

They align teams. Co-founders can see clearly: no one's pushing for aggressive marketing spend when you're still trying to find product-market fit.

Your first model doesn't need to predict the future. It needs to show the path—stage by stage—of how capital turns into progress.

This is also how you check in on progress. Your model—and divergence from it—should be the center point for meetings and updates to investors:

- What worked?
- What didn't?
- What are we going to do differently going forward?
- What assumptions are totally wrong and need to be updated?

It keeps you honest. It keeps you focused.

Your model is less about predicting numbers and more about proving judgment. Investors don't care if you're right—they care if you're rigorous and whether you understand how this business works enough to run it.

Chapter 8

Sell Me This Pen

Getting Ready to Raise

Any time you sit down with a financial advisor—or even pick an investment yourself—you'll hear two questions:

1. What's your risk tolerance?
2. What's your time horizon?

Two levers. How much pain can you take on the downside, and how long are you willing to wait for the upside?

Pitching for capital feels like you're talking to one giant category: investors. But they're not all the same. They've each got their own mix of risk appetite and patience. Use those lenses to tailor your pitch—and to know when to walk away.

The worst thing a founder can have is misaligned money that doesn't want to be part of the company anymore.

Take a look at Figure 8.1.

Let's start with an extreme: **gamblers**. I'm not saying you should take their money—you shouldn't—but they're a useful contrast to explain real investors.

Gambling is high risk, short fuse. You win or you're wiped out. Vegas wants its payoff in minutes, not years. Sports bettors stretch it to Sundays, but if the picks don't hit for a few weeks, they're broke.

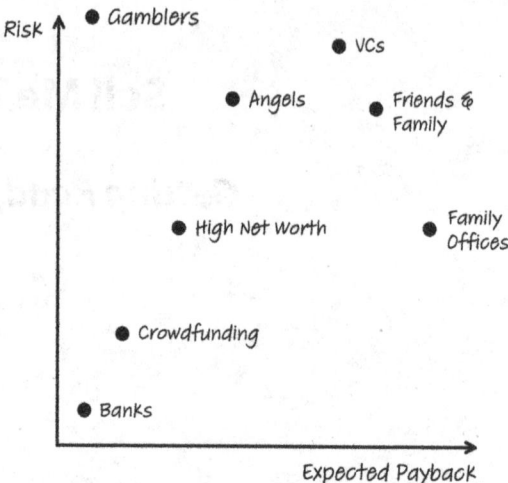

Figure 8.1 Who Takes Risk and For How Long?

Translate that mindset into startups and it's a nightmare. The last thing you need is someone banging on your door because they need their "investment" back to settle with a guy named Tony the Fist.

Wrong timeline, wrong expectations, wrong everything. If you suspect someone offering you money is really just a gambler at heart, politely decline their check.

Friends and family is the classic first stop, but also the trickiest. Ironically, some of the worst deals I've seen have come from relatives. They don't know market terms, so you wind up with bizarre valuations, strange bells and whistles, and expensive lawyers who've never done a startup deal.

And if you lose their money? Thanksgiving gets really awkward.

It all depends on where your friends and family fall on this chart. For those who are lucky enough to have the kind of network where friends can afford to write an angel check into a startup, you need to make sure they fall far to the right of the time horizon chart. This money isn't coming back anytime soon, or maybe even ever, so if they're investing out of an account they might need sometime soon, this isn't a fit.

People love to point to Jeff Bezos's parents cashing out their retirement to back Amazon. Sure, it turned into billions. But they were nearly 50—about 15 years from retirement. If Amazon had tanked, how would they have rebuilt that nest egg?

Here's the truth: if you do become the next Amazon, you'll probably take care of your parents anyway. If you don't, you'll feel like an asshole for losing their retirement.

Either way, risky bet.

The same applies to friends. Even if they can afford it, set expectations: no returns for a decade, maybe never. The worst outcome isn't losing money—it's losing a friendship.

My advice: don't hit up your best friend. Hit up your looser connections—the ones you can live without if things go sideways. You might not feel like these people are close enough to you to ask, but the worst they can do is say no.

When I raised my first fund, I sent one mass email to every contact I had. I didn't lead with an ask; I led with an offer:

> "I just closed my first fund. If you know startups looking for capital, send them my way. If you know early employees looking for roles, I'd love to meet them . . ."

Only at the end did I mention the fund itself and the type of people already backing it. If that sounded like them, great—they could raise their hand.

That single email brought in over a million dollars—from the most unexpected places. An old newsletter reader. A former intern who introduced me to his entrepreneur relatives. Nobody reacted negatively. Most ignored it. A few wished me luck.

The handful who leaned in more than paid off.

Totally worth it, but I was fortunate enough to be in privileged circles of people with investment and startup backgrounds. Not everyone has that.

If you don't, and you can't source from friends and family, then who should you be going to?

Banks? Forget it. They want payments every month—no tolerance for risk, no patience for long timelines. By the time your product ships, the interest alone could have sunk you. And don't forget the personal guarantees. They don't care if you're the next big thing—they care about rent and deposits.

Some founders opt for **crowdfunding** to get their businesses off the ground.

Crowdfunding can be a great way to get things started, but it isn't without risks.

The myth is that it scares off VCs. Not true. Just ask Oculus. They raised $2.4 million on Kickstarter in 2012, then $91 million in venture capital, and sold to Facebook two years later for $2 billion.

Like we've said time and again: Most startups aren't successful. Most don't raise VC funding. Most lose money.

So, anytime you're trying to create a rule based on what happens with startups, you're bound to arrive at something that sounds like, "This will never work if you do it this way."

It doesn't work *most of the time*. As long as you've got examples of when it does work, and you understand why it did, or why it was hard, you can address it and plan accordingly.

Keep in mind that what Oculus did was more akin to a pre-sale than a capital raise. A crowdfunding campaign could just be a bunch of people paying for something that you haven't built yet today, so that you'll have the money to get it built eventually.

That could actually be a strong signal for investors—that your consumers are willing to pay for something way in advance to ensure that you'll build it eventually. A strong showing in a pre-sale de-risks your ability to go-to market and find your customers, demonstrating strong intent.

Crowd investing is a little different. Going on a platform like Wefunder, Seedinvest, or Republic to raise means that you're, on average, pitching to a group of smaller, sometimes less sophisticated investors. That can be fine for things like consumer products where tech-focused VCs don't usually play.

When you're talking about the kind of deal that VCs would usually play in, if they pass early on and you use crowdfunding, then, yes, you're going to have to demonstrate to VCs you got over whatever reasons why others passed the first time.

Are they right all the time? No, of course not.

Crushing your goals usually makes VCs forget early passes.

Before you blame lack of VC interest on the fact that you've got a bunch of individuals from a crowd raise on your cap table, consider that the biggest issue is that you weren't a sure bet to begin with for anyone.

Let's talk about **high-net-worth individuals** and the tradeoffs of taking money from them. I don't mean professional angels—I mean rando rich people.

Dentists, if you will.

These investors can be easier to close, less sensitive to valuation, and unburdened by fund timelines. But that same lack of venture experience can cut the other way. They may push for quick payouts, struggle to see why a pre-revenue company is worth anything or hold unrealistic expectations about returns.

Before taking their money, it's critical to align on what "success" means to them, how much risk they can stomach, and whether they understand just how rare true startup wins are.

The bigger risks usually show up in execution. Non-VCs often bring in lawyers unfamiliar with standard venture terms, which drives up legal costs and can leave you with gnarly docs that scare off future investors. They may demand board seats too early or try to insert themselves into operating roles without first observing and earning trust—like a fan buying into their favorite team just to run out and play third base.

The way to mitigate this is simple: use experienced startup lawyers and stick to standard terms. Keep expectations clear, protect long-term flexibility, and make sure actual performance—not someone's cap table position—determines who gets to take on meaningful roles.

Technically, these folks are angel investors, but they rarely call themselves that. They don't market themselves as "professional angels," and it usually won't show up on their LinkedIn.

Professional angels are different. They've usually seen the movie before. They know the dynamics of high-growth startups, understand why a pre-revenue company might have real value, and often move faster because they're writing checks from their own accounts. Many bring operating or investing experience, which makes them more realistic about both risk and timelines. They also add credibility when they're respected in your sector—if the founder who won in the 1.0 version of your market says you're the 2.0 version, that endorsement carries real weight.

The flip side: professional angels are still individuals, not funds. Their capacity to follow on is limited, and you can't count on them to anchor later rounds or set valuation benchmarks the way an institutional lead can. Some lean too heavily on their operator background, tossing in product or strategy advice that doesn't fit your company's reality. And because they've built reputations in the ecosystem, they sometimes expect more access or influence than their check size justifies.

At their best, angels are supportive, founder-friendly partners who open doors and lend real advice. But you still need to set boundaries early: what level of involvement is actually helpful, how they see their role, and whether they plan to keep writing checks in future rounds. That clarity keeps the relationship scaling with the company—instead of complicating it.

Angel groups are slightly different animals. They're hit or miss. The best ones aggregate serious ex-operators. The worst ones drag you through endless screenings, forms, and meetings.

Sometimes, they're more social than professional—and if not everyone in the group is familiar with your sector, all it takes is one guy in the back saying, "I put money into a fintech startup years ago and lost everything" to kill the excitement in the room.

Venture capitalists, on the other hand, exist to take risks.

They also have different strategies for different stages—and they can always move fast if they're motivated enough—especially by FOMO (fear of missing out).

That's the whole job. They've promised their investors big returns, so they swing for home runs. Individuals? They answer only to themselves. That can make them easier—or harder. They don't need 10× returns, but they might want quicker flips, pet projects, or causes.

We'll get to those return expectations soon, but first we have to talk about **family offices**.

Family offices are like the UFOs of the investor world. No one's quite sure if they're real. Rumors of their size, shape and speed are all over the map. From what one can gather from the tales, they're able to do just about anything they want.

In real life, a family office is basically a private investment and wealth management firm set up to handle the money of one very wealthy family.

Someone once told me, *"When you meet one family office, you've met one family office."*

What they meant was that family offices have very different setups and expectations. Sometimes, the person who actually made all the money is still very actively involved. Other times, it's a group of professionals protecting, not risking, inherited money. Their investment risk appetite and time horizons can differ wildly.

It's best to ask as many questions as you need to assess whether this is a good use of everyone's time.

In terms of size, a family office tends to have at least $100–250 million in investable assets, because below that it's hard to justify the cost of hiring full-time staff. Be careful, though—because not everyone who "works for a family office" is actually on staff.

Saying that you work for a family office can get you into a lot of cool places.

Remember Anna Delvey?

She was a con artist with a comically bad fake accent who posed as a wealthy German heiress in New York City. Between 2013 and 2017, she scammed friends, hotels, and financial institutions out of hundreds of thousands of dollars by faking connections to elite wealth and promising access to a nonexistent fortune.

Claiming to have a "family office" behind her was a shortcut to making herself look like she belonged in the same circles as the ultra rich. If you say you're connected to one, it suggests you're backed by patient money, you move in elite networks, and you don't need to answer basic financial questions.

For Anna, it was a way to cover gaps.

When someone pressed her about who was paying her bills, she could invoke a "family office" as a kind of vague, untouchable authority—legit-sounding but hard to verify.

Sometimes, people say they're "working with a family office" because a family office actually did say, "If you see any good deals, please send them my way."

This is a pretty loose connection. You shouldn't spend a lot of time with these folks unless you've verified they've made intros that resulted in successful raises.

Other times, they're completely full of shit and the only good outcome will be getting to play yourself in the Netflix series about the next Anna Delvey–like fraudster.

About Those VCs

If you want to understand why VCs say "no" so often, start here:

The outcomes they need aren't just rare—they're mythical.

The bar isn't high because they're being jerks. It's high because almost nothing they fund ever gets big enough to matter.

Forget billion-dollar "unicorns"—just getting to any level of venture-scale is wildly unlikely. You can't build a nice, useful little company and hope it magically turns into a unicorn.

You have to design for bigness from the start.

You have to pick a market that can support a billion-dollar outcome. You have to build with the kind of ambition and velocity that even has a shot at attracting capital at scale and lots of attention.

Otherwise, you're asking for venture outcomes while building a lifestyle business in disguise.

Here's some context on how rare it is to just sell a company for *only* $250 million (a quarter-corn?).

Think about running a marathon.

You don't just jog around your neighborhood for a few months and hope one day you'll stumble into mile 26.2.

You pick a date. You follow a plan. You train like hell.

You might think running 26.2 miles sounds pretty amazing—but not unbelievable. You probably know a few people who've done it. Maybe you have—about a million people around the world run a marathon each year.

Now, breaking four hours in a marathon? That's a solid feat. But it's doable—around 40% of marathoners (including me!) hit that mark. Maybe you know someone. Maybe it's you.

Congrats.

What about three hours?

Now we're in rarified air. Only 4% finish that fast—just under a seven-minute mile pace. That's about 20,000 people per year worldwide.

Pretty special.

And yet—*still not close to winning.* A 3:00 marathon puts you in only 2,000th place in New York City's annual race.

The very *top* finishers? They're averaging under five minutes per mile for over 26 miles straight.

For context, my fastest single mile ever is 5:34 and I'm a pretty decent athlete.

Only about 300 people in the world do a sub-five-minute pace for an entire marathon each year.

That's still 2–3x the number of founders who exit for $250 million or more in a given year and for most VCs, that's just barely big enough.

If you're a founder spectating or even running in your local city's marathon—just remember, actual venture-sized startup success is like having a real shot at winning this race.

Daunting, right?

But someone *does* win. *Why can't it be you? It should be you!*

Why is $250 million and up such a big deal? Wouldn't investors be happy with less?

Venture Math

Let's say you run a $50 million fund. You lead the seed and do your pro-rata in the Series A, winding up with ~10%.

To return just half the fund, you need a $250 million outcome—and that's if everything goes right: no down rounds, no aggressive liquidation preferences, and no dilution you couldn't follow.

And to return the whole fund? You'd need two of those. For a 2×? Four. And that's the bare minimum to stay in business.

You might be asking, "But a VC fund does far more than four deals, no? What's happening with all the rest of the companies?"

If an investor is writing checks into the first round, most of those deals are going absolutely nowhere. They're backing two people and a duct-taped prototype—one that is probably ahead of where the market is, but without a big budget.

Hard things are hard and even though these startups might've been the best five or six out of 2,000 deals that investor saw this year, at least half of them will be absolute zeros.

Between the flameouts and the winners, you might get your money back on some, maybe a double or triple on others. One might get you back five times your money—but about 75% of your return is going to come from just 10% or so of the portfolio. That's the "power law" distribution of a VC fund. Just a few deals will be such big outcomes that they swamp the returns from every other deal in the fund—so they need to be really, really big.

For firms that are over $50 million, they need to be even larger, to return all the additional money investors put into that fund to make it so big. That's why investors ask questions about getting to a billion-dollar "unicorn" outcome—because without it, it's really difficult to make that 3–5× return on your $100–200 million fund and beyond.

What do those companies even look like?

The answer is, frustratingly, "it depends."

Sometimes, a company becomes so strategically important to industry giants in a platform war that the cost of not owning it outweighs how little revenue it's actually making.

That was Oculus in 2014.

They had no revenue. Fewer than 100 employees. No commercially available product.

Facebook paid $2 billion.

Sounds stupid, right?

But it wasn't totally out of nowhere—especially in context. Around that time, big tech was placing platform bets. Google had paid $1.6 billion for YouTube years earlier—despite it bleeding money, facing massive copyright issues, and being dismissed as "a site for cat videos."

What Google saw was user growth. YouTube was becoming the default video platform, and by 2014, it was generating $4 billion a year and ranking as the number-two search engine.

Facebook made a similar move with Instagram, paying $1 billion just two years before the Oculus deal. Instagram was mobile-native, fast-growing, and better positioned for the mobile shift Facebook was struggling with. The acquisition helped answer investors who were worried Facebook couldn't win on mobile.

Both deals were stock-heavy and cost about 1% of the company's market cap.

Oculus followed the same logic. Virtual worlds were hyped as the next big platform shift. Oculus had best-in-class optics, an oversubscribed Kickstarter, a loyal developer community, and a ton of buzz. Even with no product, it looked like the future. Facebook didn't want to miss it—especially with rumors that Google was sniffing around virtual reality.

They thought they were buying the next iPhone.

Instead, they got a really expensive pair of ski goggles no one wanted to wear. Cool tech, tiny audience, clunky hardware—and almost no one wanted to strap into the metaverse. Billions later, Oculus is a footnote swallowed by Meta, its founders long gone.

You might call the Oculus founder lucky (which he would answer to, since his name is, in fact, Palmer Luckey), because he never actually built a big business—but what he did build was an idea big enough that Facebook thought they needed to spend billions of dollars getting out ahead of it.

Just think about how much vision, ambition, and hype you'd need—on just a prototype—to get a company like Facebook to spend billions.

That's almost harder than building the business itself.

If you do want to do it the old-fashioned way, depending on your growth, there are some ballpark metrics around the size of company you'd need to build in order to turn your dream into a billion-dollar exit.

If you were a SaaS company, you probably need to get up to about $100 million in revenue, with 30–50% growth and 70–80% gross margins. For a consumer subscription company, you might be talking even higher revenues, but your stickiness and LTV/CAC (long-term value/customer acquisition cost) ratios matter a lot.

E-commerce companies get lower multiples—so you might be talking about a quarter to a half a billion dollars in revenue before anyone suggested paying a billion dollars to acquire you, given their lower margins.

A lot of it comes down to the market you're in and how much bigger players that can afford to pay that much (of which there are few) consider you to be the key to unlocking far more than they paid (or preventing someone else from doing so).

So, when a VC asks about your market size, or your go-to-market, or how you scale—what they're really asking is:

Does this even have the raw ingredients to get big enough to matter?

Whether you're aiming for $100 million in SaaS revenue or hoping to sell on vision alone, the bar for bigness isn't just high . . .

It's intentional. It's structural.

And if you're not building like you know that, you're not building for venture.

Pitching 101

I once watched an experienced head of sales give a talk at a growth-stage startup. He was a little older, calm, and deliberate. He opened by telling us exactly what would happen in the next 35 minutes:

Five minutes on his company and customers—just enough context to understand their sales approach.

Twenty minutes on the three biggest lessons he'd learned scaling four companies past $100 million in revenue—each with a tactical takeaway any founder could use.

Ten minutes for questions.

Then he asked, "Does that sound like a good use of everyone's time?"

We all nodded.

Only later did I realize: he'd just used one of the oldest sales tactics in the book—getting everyone to agree to be sold to before he even started. That simple framing made us more open to his message. And that was just one of a dozen subtle moves he used.

The best fundraisers understand this instinctively. They don't see sales as sleazy cold calls or trickery. They see it for what it is: a repeatable process that moves people from "I've never heard of you" to "Shut up and take my money."

And fundraising? It's just sales where your "product" is equity and your "customer" is an investor buying returns.

Fundraising is sales with a fancier jacket and it requires a process to work.

Here's your crash course:

> Rookies think, "If they have money, I should pitch them." Pros know you need an ICP—Ideal Customer Profile—just like in sales.

That means:

- They invest at your stage.
- They invest in your category.
- They invest in your geography.

If they've done nothing but Series B fintech in Europe and you're a U.S. seed-stage healthtech company, stop wasting everyone's time. If they're a real estate family office that has never invested in tech before, it's a long shot at best—especially if they can't be a customer of that tech because it isn't real estate tech.

The key is qualifying before you pitch. Track who's worth chasing. Make a list that has an actual shot of converting and treat your pipeline like a funnel.

Every investor conversation is a stage with a % chance of closing—and you need volume at the top. If you want two term sheets, you might need:

- 100 leads (target list) →
- 40–60 first meetings →
- 10–20 second meetings →
- 5–8 partnership meetings →
- 2–3 final offers

The real mistake? Too few meetings early, waiting weeks for "maybe" feedback, then having to start from scratch. Fill the top. Push out slow movers. Keep the good ones in motion.

Know what each step means (see Figure 8.2).

As for the story, your pitch isn't your deck—it's the conversation arc. Don't just read the deck to people and make sure you know the difference between a deck you send and a deck you read.

Fundraising Stage Progression

Stage #	Fundraising Stage (Sales Equivalent)	Description	% Chance of Closing
1	Target List/Prospecting ("Leads Generated")	You've identified investors who actually write checks at your stage, in your sector, and in your geography. No contact yet.	~1–2%
2	Initial Outreach Sent ("Contacted")	Warm intro, conference meeting, or cold email sent. They've seen a teaser or know the category.	~1–2%
3	First Meeting Booked ("Discovery Call")	You've got a call/Zoom/in-person booked to walk through high-level story. They didn't pass.	~3–5%
4	First Meeting Done—Interested ("Qualified Lead")	They've heard your pitch, asked relevant questions, and want to learn more. This is your true pipeline now.	~10%
5	Second/Follow-Up Meeting ("Solution Fit")	You're going deeper on product, traction, market. Possibly meeting more of their team. They're evaluating you seriously.	~15–20%
6	Partner/Full Team Meeting ("Proposal Stage")	The whole partnership is in the room. They're looking for holes in the story and internal alignment.	~25–40%
7	Diligence/Reference Checks ("Negotiation")	They're digging into your data room, calling customers, checking references. They're deciding whether to offer terms.	~20–25%
8	Verbal Commit/Term Sheet Issued ("Closed Won Pending")	They've said they're in, but you haven't signed yet. Deal can still blow up here if something spooks them or round dynamics shift.	~70%
9	Signed & Wired ("Closed Won")	Money in the bank.	100%

Figure 8.2 Fundraising Pipeline Stages

People can read faster than you can speak to the deck. There's nothing that's more of a buzzkill than watching someone read a page you've already finished.

You also need pre-loaded answers to the most common objections. In fact, you should bring up the objections before they do—or even ask them for their concerns before you start.

Call out the game. Ask, "Why'd you take this meeting and why are you going to pass on us?" before you start. This way, you have an information advantage going in and you know what objections you have to get over if you're going to turn them.

Basically, every word spoken in that meeting should be strategic and intentional. You should be coaxing information out of investors that helps you understand where their mind is at and gives you the keys to unlock an investment.

On your end, you should be diffusing objections before they happen and laying down a breadcrumb trail back to the inevitable conclusion that they should investment.

If you're just making it up as you go, answering whatever questions they throw at you, you're dead in the water.

Creating FOMO Without Getting Your Bluff Called

A deal with no deadline never closes. Somehow, you've got to push an investor to a yes or a no sooner rather than later, even though you don't feel like you have any leverage. That doesn't mean faking demand—it means controlling the time you spend per investor.

Try this out:

"For a pre-seed round, most investors we've spoken to can get to a yes/no in three weeks. Does that seem reasonable? If so, here's a proposed three-week process with go/no-go milestones. If we can't get to an agreement by the end, we'll part ways professionally."

Here's how it might look:

Three-Week Investor Decision Timeline

(For a pre-seed round—with go/no-go milestones and stakeholder alignment)

Week 1—High-Level Fit

- Intro call + 10-slide deck
- Ask: "Who else should be looped in if this is a fit so far?"
- Go/No-Go #1

Week 2—Deep Dive

- Product, traction, competition deep dive with all stakeholders
- Data room access
- Check for missing decision-makers
- Go/No-Go #2

Week 3—Final Alignment

- Partner meeting/all decision-makers present
- Final questions + decision deadline email
- Go/No-Go #3

Stick to it: the power comes from actually following through.

You don't lie. You don't fake demand. But you run your process in a tight window so conversations overlap and investors feel the clock ticking.

Make sure every meeting ends with a next step and a date.

Not: "I'll send you more info," or "We'll be in touch."

Try: "Let's schedule the partner meeting for next Wednesday." Or "If that Tuesday call works out, can we get a partner meeting for next Wednesday?"

If an investor is interested, they'll move forward quickly. If they drag their feet, they're either not sold or not serious.

- Keep a simple customer relationship management (even a Google Sheet) tracking:
  - Stage in process
  - Key takeaways from meeting
  - Next step date

Cut off what isn't moving fast enough and let them know it:

"It was great getting to know you, but we didn't hear any follow-up questions after the meeting. Plus, you missed my note about having a next step happening by the end of the week. It seems you're not as enthusiastic about the business as some other investors, so I'd move for us to pause our conversations right now so we can focus on more interested investors."

See how fast they come jumping back into the process.:)

Even the investor who eventually says yes won't agree with everything you say. If nothing else, you want something of a spirited debate. When an investor pushes back in a meeting, that's not rejection—that's engagement.

They care enough to argue.
A good sales move: Feel, Felt, Found.

- Feel: "I understand why you'd be worried about that . . ."
- Felt: "A lot of other investors initially felt the same way . . ."
- Found: ". . . but they found our retention data eliminated the concern."

Defensiveness kills deals. Curiosity and data save them.
End every meeting with:

"If this fits your thesis, is there anything else you'd need to get to a decision?"

It's a respectful nudge, not a hard shove, because your time is valuable.

Coffee chats with no next steps are fine when you're not raising, but when you are, they're a distraction.

Batch your meetings. Keep your deck tight and ready. And don't rebuild your pitch from scratch every time unless you've learned something big enough to change it for everyone.

Who Controls the Purse Strings?

In sales, there's the user and the budget holder.
In VC, there's:

- The non-partner associate/analyst/principal—your champion or potentially a distraction who has no juice in the process. Each one is different and worth referencing other founders on to see if they actively participated in the deal closing process.
- The partner is your main buyer and. . .
- The partnership is the budget committee.

You need talking points for all three—well-organized market and due diligence info so that the associate can write up a memo, solid confidence-inducing vision for the partner, and objection answers so that partner can sell it to their firm.

Pull the Rip Cord

Don't be afraid to walk away. Bad-fit customers waste your team's time. Bad-fit investors waste your life.

If they're slow-rolling you, negotiating in bad faith, or pushing terms you can't live with—move on. The right deal will move faster.

Fundraising isn't a mystery. It's just sales.

Run it like a sales process and you'll move faster, get better terms, and avoid dying in "we're still thinking about it" purgatory.

The founders who close rounds don't have magic charisma. They just know how to work a funnel, manage a clock, and create the conditions where "yes" is the obvious answer.

For the Love of the Raise

Imagine sitting in a room full of people who doubt you and your idea, waiting to hear your pitch.

They're skeptical that what you're attempting to do is possible, a good idea, or that you're the right person to do it.

Nightmare or inspiration?

If it's a nightmare, you need to do something about it.

You can't raise unless you love raising.

I've never met anyone who feared scrutiny who succeeded in the fundraising process. If you don't learn to love it, you're never going to dive deep enough into it in order to figure it out. Any athlete will tell you that they couldn't be motivated to get better at a sport unless they really loved it. If you don't find fundraising a fascinating step in the process and if you're not curious about what's inside an investors head, how you're coming off—and really obsessive about every step in the process, it's hard to see how you're going to improve, especially as the stakes get higher with bigger rounds along the way.

These are people whose sole job is to weed you out—to come up with a reason to say no.

They've got 2,000 opportunities to look at in order to get down to the two, three, four, or five they work on this year. The quicker they can get to a no, tearing apart your entire pitch, the faster they can make it through this insurmountable pile.

Tough questions and skepticism are what it's all about. If they were optimistic, they'd have too many "this could work" deals to choose from and they'd never make an investment.

That isn't going to change, so you need to figure out a way to not only deal with it—but to thrive in that environment.

Let's start with your own confidence level. Are you a naturally confident person? Can you hold your own in a tooth-and-nail argument or do you fold when you're feeling like the other person doesn't believe you or fundamentally disagrees?

And where does that come from?

I'm a huge believer that everyone should go to therapy so that you can have a coach for your emotional state and well-being. Just like hiring a GTM advisor, or a technical resource, therapy is a founder tool. It helps you understand what triggers you, what shuts you down, and how to stay grounded when everything is on fire.

A therapist helps you unpack the baggage you carry into every pitch—your self-image, your confidence, and your reflexes around certain types of people.

There are some people who, no matter how much work they do to understand a problem and come up with a great solution, have a deep-seated insecurity. Working on your pitch deck more isn't going to solve that—but working with a professional to unlock everything about why you and your emotions work the way they do will. You might not figure things out exactly, but it's one of the many ways you can be as prepared as possible to start a company. You'll maintain better composure in the face of all types of stress—from the stress of getting eviscerated in the very worst pitch you'll ever deliver to discovering the well of resilience you'll need to step up for the next one.

It will help you treat your co-founder better, your employees and get out ahead of your blind spots before they sink your company.

They'll also help you be less defensive—which is incredibly helpful in a fundraising process. When you're defensive, you comes off as thin-skinned, easily rattled, and unprepared. Do you think these are founder qualities investors are rushing to back?

Dealing with scrutiny is a skill to be practiced. You don't need to like being doubted. You need to learn how to use it to your advantage. Start with your friendliest skeptics. Ask your smartest friend to poke holes in your pitch. Talk to 10 customers in a row who don't buy.

Train the reflex.

Instead of defending, listen.

Then improve.

An investor is sitting across the table from you trying to imagine working together, solving problems no one else has had to solve yet. They're hoping that you bring as much information as possible to a discussion, while being able to admit where things aren't working and where your knowledge is coming up short. They're expecting you to seek out answers from your team, your advisors, from them, and, most importantly, from potential customers in the market.

That involves being comfortable in your own skin, confident that you have value, in your accomplishments to date, and in your potential. If you're too busy trying to be someone you aren't, someone who has all the answers when they don't, that's going to come through and make you look too emotionally fragile to run this gauntlet.

Sometimes, the issue isn't inside you—it's in your path to the idea. At some point, you have to admit that you weren't as prepared as you could have been, and that the skepticism of the idea is actually well-founded.

If you don't accept the fact that investors might be right to turn you down, it's hard to see how you're ever going to either improve something that still has potential, or dump the idea that is eating up your peak earning years.

You should look at investors scrutinizing your plan as them doing you a favor. If they rightfully tear it apart with good questions that you can't really answer well, they're doing you a favor. They're saving you from a bad idea, or they're saving a good idea from an unprepared founder.

How to Talk Big

"Jerry . . . remember. It's not a lie if you believe it."

That famous George Costanza line from *Seinfeld* satirizes the mental gymnastics people use to justify dishonesty. It captures how self-deception blurs the line between truth and fiction, especially in high-stakes situations like sales, politics, or startup pitches.

Just where is that line when it comes to startup pitches?

Here's a thought exercise:

What's the most obviously impossible startup you could imagine?

A time machine startup—that's a total fraud, right?

I would argue that it's only fraudulent if you're selling certainty—not possibility.

Think about this pitch as if it was modeled after deep-tech efforts that began as science fiction—like private space travel, quantum computing, or OpenAI's early AGI research.

Team and Hiring Strategy

We are assembling an interdisciplinary team of world-class talent to explore the scientific and engineering frontiers of temporal mechanics, causality, and exotic spacetime manipulation. While the development of a functioning time machine is currently considered beyond the limits of known physics, we are building a research-first company modeled after successful deep-tech efforts that began with "impossible" ideas—like private space travel or AGI.

Translation: We know this is really hard, but if anyone is going to do it, it's us.

Our core hires include:

- **Theoretical Physicist (Relativity and Quantum Gravity):** Explore the plausibility of time loops, wormholes, and exotic spacetime models.
- **Experimental Physicist (Quantum Systems):** Design and run lab tests on time symmetry, entanglement, and causal anomalies.
- **Applied Mathematician (Topology and Systems):** Model time as a dimension and simulate spacetime folding and stability.
- **Quantum Computing Engineer:** Use quantum systems to simulate time evolution and branching paths.
- **Mechanical Engineer (Extreme Environments):** Design physical systems for handling local spacetime distortions.
- **Ethicist and Legal Futurist:** Map the ethical and legal challenges of time manipulation and causal disruption.

Translation: We understand the problem enough to know what kind of team it would take to be successful.

What They'll Do:

- Develop and test theoretical models of temporal mechanics.
- Simulate time-bound anomalies and edge conditions using quantum systems and numerical methods.
- Publish and peer-review novel research expanding the boundaries of time perception and manipulation.
- Build tools and experimental setups for detecting temporal asymmetries or feedback loops.
- Work with external labs and universities on foundational physics collaboration.
- Create thought experiments and policy frameworks for when (not if) breakthroughs occur.

How We Frame the Mission

We are not claiming to build a working time machine next year. We're building the first credible commercial research platform for time travel exploration, the way SpaceX was not about launching rockets on day one, but building the talent, tooling, and culture for the impossible to become inevitable.

I mean, this actually sounds like the kind of thing that you wouldn't be surprised if Sam Altman started working on tomorrow alongside a $100 million check from A16Z.

All of the sudden, time itself would seem like a bigger platform to be working on than AI, which would seem "so 2024."

But remember: just 10 years ago, OpenAI was a vague nonprofit with a mission, not a business plan.

"OpenAI is a non-profit artificial intelligence research company. Our goal is to advance digital intelligence in the way that is most likely to benefit humanity as a whole, unconstrained by a need to generate financial return."

Who would have thought that in a decade, OpenAI would go from a nonprofit research experiment to the most consequential platform shift since the internet—rewriting the stack of intelligence itself.

The most important unlock is that you're not pitching what's likely to happen. You're pitching what's *possible*.

When you raise capital, you're selling tickets to a very big future. It's not a reward for what you've done in the past—even if you'd like it to be.

That would feel more honest, I'm sure.

While I appreciate the sentiment behind "judge me on my results," the reality for most founders pre-funding is that if you haven't raised money yet, you probably haven't accomplished anything compelling yet.

Don't get me wrong, bootstrapping your way to actually creating a product out of nothing, getting someone to use it, pay for it, and getting anywhere close to breaking even is an amazing feat—but those are things that lots of people are able to do, and very few of those people make it to VC-sized exits.

That begs the question of how a founder is ever supposed to get comfortable talking about it with confidence if it's so rare and unlikely—and where's the line between being aggressive and being dishonest?

Sandbagging

What's most likely to happen is that your company goes out of business. After all, that's what happens to most startups, even the ones that get funded.

Given that your pitch desk probably doesn't say this—that you're going to face plant after burning up all your investor's cash in a blaze of glory—*you're already suspending reality.*

Why stop there?

Why bother essentially saying, "We're quite confident that we're going to beat the odds and not lose your money, but we don't feel comfortable going a step further and state that we can deliver a really compelling financial exit for you."

It's a really odd level of false precision that also somehow lacks ambition.

"Breakthrough Mediocrity."

Sounds like one of those fake band names.

They opened for Modest Mouse at Hammerstein. Great logo. Mid set. (Their big hit was "Runway Projections (But Conservative)".)

Is it possible that your company winds up being something more? If you actually get to the point of having a product in the market, is it possible that customers actually like it? Is it possible that you figure out growth?

Unlikely? Sure.

But is it "impossible"?

Definitely not.

Belief isn't the absence of doubt. It's the willingness to plan anyway.

"So how do you know if your 'impossible' pitch is actually investable?"

Try running it through this sanity check:

- Is there a team out there that's done this before you can talk to, learn from, or maybe even hire?
- Does your plan require capital in line with what others have raised?
- Can you sketch a plan that builds realistically quarter over quarter?

If it's impossible, you shouldn't even be working on it—but if you can check these boxes, this kind of "possible" is all a VC is really asking for.

VCs know the odds. That's why they invest in a portfolio. They know that half of their investments are going to fail.

What they really need to understand is that for the ones that make it, do those successes have a *chance* at returning multiples of the entire fund?

If you can't disprove it, the answer has to be yes.

Is it impossible that my theoretical time machine startup could make some headway? Most people couldn't prove it—and that's where the confidence has to come from. It's a lie when you *know* something won't happen. With a team like the one I assembled and the self-awareness to know that we're attempting a really hard thing, without any grandstanding impossible to fulfill promises, all we're doing is being ambitious while staying on the right side of the line of honest intentions.

I remember investing in a company and trying to convince a group of angels to join me. The company processed organic waste and turned it into useable products—cleaners, soil additives, etc. One of the angels asked me, "What's the exit for a company like this?"

I very confidently said, "Well, an acquisition or an IPO."

They responded, "You think this is going to be a public company??"

That's not what I was saying—but it's what they heard. I wasn't promising an IPO. I was reminding them that, sometimes, garbage turns into gold.

"Can you prove to me that it can't be? They process garbage. Is there not enough garbage in the world for them to grow that big?" I asked.

Again, it's not about what's likely. It's about what's conceivably real—and worth betting on.

All Gas, No Brakes

So how aggressive should you be in your ambition when you pitch?

Try the "Step on the Gas Test." How far can you stretch your plan before reality breaks?

Imagine an investor turns to you in the middle of your not-so-ambitious pitch and asks, "How would you double these projections?"

"What would actually be involved?"

"How would you do it if I gave you the money?"

If the answer is, "Of course we could do it—we'd do X, Y, and Z," then that's what you should be pitching. You should be asking for the amount of money that it takes you to accomplish that and building the plan accordingly.

Now do it again.

Could you double your projections again without breaking from reality? I'm not saying it wouldn't be hard—but is it just total fantasy land or is it *possible?*

Push those numbers until that thought experiment breaks—when you say to yourself, "That's probably too much to attempt—things would break before they had a chance to succeed," or, "No one would ever write us that check for that much money upfront—and I wouldn't even write us that check if I had the money."

Then, you know you've maxed out your plan. That's what you should actually be pitching—and you should be confident about it based on your knowledge of the space—of what assumptions are real and what are totally made up.

What's really interesting when you plan for your highest potential is that if you do that year after year, you're bound to get to some very big outcomes six-, seven-, eight-plus years down the line thanks to the magic of compounding—growing larger off a large base.

Here's what it could actually look like:

If you get to $1 million, with the right investment, could you do $3 million the next year?

That doesn't seem so impossible, does it? You probably got to $1 million with a very small team. You wouldn't even need to add that many more people to reasonably triple that given what you did with your skeleton crew.

Now, if you get to $3 million, could you get to $8 million the year after that? You tripled the year before—2.5× doesn't feel so wild now.

Now, once you're an $8 million company, growing to $100 million in annual revenues in the six years after that just requires around 50% annual growth—not even doubling every year or anything close to that.

Do you think it's possible to build a plan like that?

Of course it is—especially when you're doing $30 million a year. Each step of the way is going to feel more and more likely because of everything you accomplished up until this point.

When you're barely at $100,000 in revenues, $100 million feels insane to say, but you have to imagine that your $3 million revenue future self could find their way to $8 million, then $12 million after that, and so on and so on.

That's the second big unlock—that not only are we talking about what's possible versus what's likely, but that we're going to root the whole thing in a thoughtful plan. We're not just pulling numbers out of our butts—we're making educated guesses based on research and the best practices of those who have come before you.

Too often, founders aren't talking to other founders who have done it. Saying that you can get to $50 or $100 million a year in revenue won't seem like made up bullshit when you've talked to multiple people who have done it before and they walk you through all the knowledge they unlocked along the way.

When you hear about all the boneheaded mistakes they made when they first started out—far worse than anything you've done so far—things start to seem a lot more believable.

Down to the Penny Doesn't Impress

Also, you need to set your level of granularity appropriately. If you're quoting third-year revenue down to the dollar ("My model says $3,342,231."), then you are actually being *dishonest*. You don't actually know that's going to be the number—so don't try to get more accurate than is reasonable. Clean, directionally correct round numbers with lots of zeros behind them keep the focus high-level and the detail at an appropriate level—and they signal that, of course, nothing is exact.

This is another place where underrepresented founders, especially women, fall right into a bias trap. Both male and female VCs already have a predisposition (thanks society!) to not think of women as bold, big-picture thinkers willing to take on big risks.

The moment you start rummaging through your model to get the exact number versus just ballparking it, you reenforce the stereotype.

Would I hire this woman as my CFO? Yes!

Can she take the big risks necessary to drive this company to $100 million in revenue? I'd ask her, but she's still searching through the spreadsheet to tell me whether it's $0.47 or $0.48 as the final two digits of her year seven EBITDA (earnings before interest, taxes, depreciation, and amortization).

It's tricky to constantly switch back and forth between operator mode, where being exacting comes in handy and fundraiser mode broad strokes is the language of visionaries, but that's the language of venture for better or worse.

Chapter 9

These Are Not the Droids You're Looking For

The Pitch

Are you an outsider or an insider in the venture capital world?

My question to you if you're an outsider is . . . why?

Be an Insider from Day One

You're working on a startup idea in a space where there have hopefully been at least some innovative companies, or at least the model has worked in another vertical.

Why aren't you a student of these other companies—and not just a student—*the* student?

You should be emailing the founders, asking questions about their most recent podcast appearance or conference panel, talking to former employees of those companies about the good, the bad and the ugly, and researching why customers bought their product.

When you're across the table from an investor and they flippantly throw out that, "This is like Company X that failed" you should know all the reasons why, in fact, Company X failed for some other reason and this was actually the part that was working.

How did you know that? Because you've already interviewed a half dozen of Company X's former engineers.

What does any of this have to do with fundraising?

The investors who want to make new investments in this space are putting themselves out there to attract founders just like you. They're marketing their firms, speaking on panels at industry conferences and writing their thoughts on the space. They're trying to meet you to get a look at what you think is the next big thing—so the fact that you haven't met them yet is really on you.

Plus, I find myself skeptical of a founder who swears they've got the next big thing, but somehow has never run into, talked to, read the writing of, or even heard of very investors who are looking for that next big thing in their category.

The only way you can be sure you've got something truly big is if you're close enough to the middle of your industry and so completely in the flow that you can see *everything* innovative that is going on—including the folks financing the change and the founders they've already backed.

If you're not seeing investors and founders around you, you're on the outside looking in—and I don't see how you can state for a fact that no one else is working on this with a better approach.

Use investors to vet and develop your idea.

You might say, "Well, I haven't started fundraising yet and that's why I'm not yet talking to investors," but that positions building connections with investors at the wrong end of the process.

Connecting with investors shouldn't be the thing you do at the end of all of the research, prototyping, testing, and pitch development. It's not the thing you do *after* you crush your goals.

It should be one of the first things you do—even before you're set on what the idea is. Investors have an information advantage. They've seen most of the attempts at building something in this space—many of whom never even saw the light of day because they failed.

You can learn from these failures—or, if nothing else, get a sense of what questions an investor is going to ask when you're really ready.

You should understand their skepticism ahead of time. You should know that things they're willing to accept at face value and what things they need to see you accomplish before they're willing to believe it's possible.

That's how you can most efficiently spend whatever capital you've bootstrapped into the company or what friends and family money you've spent—so you can use it to prove the thing standing in the way of getting a check.

You might even learn that they're so in love with your idea and the fact that *you*, with your fantastic background and stellar team, are working on it that they'll fund you on the spot before you've proven anything.

You won't know until you reach out to them—and the best and most efficient way to do that is to start building your lists through other founders.

Founders help founders. Great founders make great mentors.

I don't mean *any* founders. I mean the founders that are clearly winning—raising the next round or two ahead of you and whose companies are getting great press coverage. Not only do they know investors because they've been out pitching, but as an attractive company, they're also getting lots of inbound. They'll be able to share their investor list faster than you'll be able to attempt to research any of the various paid investor databases that are out there.

Here are tactical steps to take to use other founders to help build your top of funnel.

Start with Interviews

I already told you about Harry Stebbings, who, at 18, with no VC connections, no podcasting experience, and a cheap mic, started cold-emailing VCs and inviting them on *The Twenty Minute VC* podcast. Not to pitch them. Not to impress them. Just to learn.

They said yes.

Not all of them, obviously—but a few. And that was enough to get the flywheel turning.

This is how you get into the flow of where investors and the founders they've backed who have investor networks play. It doesn't even need to be a full-blown podcast. You can use simple tools like Riverside to publish interviews and highlights directly to LinkedIn or in newsletters.

If you keep showing up with thoughtful questions and share what you're learning, you will attract the kind of people who want to help. Founders spend so much time trying to "get in the room"—but creating a space for others to fill is often the most effective way to earn your seat.

Swing for the Fences

Who are the bellwether unicorns and massive successes in your space—the 5- to 10-year-old companies with the eye-popping valuations that are rumored to be going IPO? Their founders and C-level leaders would make great guests if you can get them. Offer to fill a room for them if you can't just do a 1:1 interview for LinkedIn or a podcast. Maybe partner with a school or a venture capital firm—or some other tech organization.

Ask them great questions, allow them to tell their story, and then follow up with yours. Share your hypothesis that there's something new and great to be built. Take their questions and their skepticism seriously and let them suggest to you who the most knowledgeable investors they know in the space are—especially the ones still interested in investing in this area.

After you talk to the big names, work your way down. Who has successfully raised the kind of round you're looking to raise in your space? They'll accept an interview for different reasons—because they're trying to get on more people's radars.

What's great about talking to founders who just went through it is that they know how hard it was for them, so they'll be likely to share the information they gathered and make intros on your behalf if you impress them enough. They'll tell you which investors to steer clear of and who were the most helpful.

Peer Groups FTW!

There are lots of WhatsApp and other networking groups for every industry vertical you can imagine. A lot of founders and aspiring and current VCs find it in their professional best interest to curate communities of startup folks. Being in them is like going to graduate business school—surrounding yourself with ambitious and well-connected folks also actively building out their networks.

Leverage them for feedback on your pitch as well as to source names you haven't surface yet. Ideally, these are curated groups—so the people you're learning from have at least accomplished a little more than you have up to this point.

Once you've gotten enough suggestions for who to pitch, you want to qualify investor leads. Instead of attempting to "sell," you want to eliminate as many names as possible. Start by sending out feelers either directly and through your network that give people a reason to say no.

What's the worst part of your company and the pitch? I don't mean the worst part to everyone, but to some people who will be an automatic no. Who doesn't do any hardware, or won't touch anything connected to real estate? Who's a hard no on pre-revenue?

Whatever it is that would get you a no should be paired with the most compelling aspects of why someone would want to talk to you.

Amazing team working in a huge, compelling space to do a really hard thing is at a super super early stage.

Anyone who looks past how hard this is and who doesn't care about what stage you're at that loves this space should be your first conversations. Those are going to be the best early conversations before you even get to actually pitching—and you should make sure you stay in touch with them as the idea develops.

Here are some additional basics to qualify the right investors:

- Check size match: Don't waste time pitching a $250,000 raise to a fund with a $10,000,000 minimum.
- Stage fit: Some firms say "pre-seed" but mean post-revenue. Look at their actual portfolio, not just the website copy. Ask qualifying questions like, "Have you done any pre-revenue deals in the last year?"
- Category interest: Have they invested in your vertical or something adjacent recently? If their last fintech investment was in 2017, they're probably not active there anymore.
- Pacing and bandwidth: Are they actively deploying from a fresh fund, or are they in year four of a vintage that's winding down?
- Cross-reference this with what recent founders say: Are they seeing this investor around deals? Getting fast decisions? Or hearing crickets?

Treat that first call like a reverse pitch. Here are some high-signal questions to mix into the chat:

"What made you excited about [a recent investment]?"
→ Does your company resonate in the same way?
"At what point do you usually invest in a company like ours?"
→ Forces them to clarify their real bar for traction/team/market.
"What are the most common reasons you pass on companies in this space?"
→ This surfaces objections early.

"If you were bullish on something like this, what else would you want to see?"

→ Helps you understand how far off you are—or whether they're just not into it.

If they waffle or overuse generic platitudes ("you're too early," "not a fit right now")—they're hedging. Push (gently) for specificity.

"Too early? What haven't I done yet that you're willing to bet that I won't be able to do?"

When they say they're going back to their team, understand whether they're going back to champion a potential investment or pull in resources to form a diligence team, or they're just doing it to cover their ass when you IPO and someone notices your deal was in their CRM way back when.

Understand why if it's the CYA (cover your ass) thing. "Why aren't you pulling partners into this?"

Ask the question directly.

Take the feedback seriously, figure out what you can do about it, and try to find someone willing to take that same risk when they're not.

A Seed by Any Other Name

Once they've figured out how much to raise, a lot of founders get wrapped around the axle on what to call the raise.

Is it a pre-seed? Seed? Angel? Friends and family?

What the hell is a "mango seed"?

Don't worry, I've got you. You can rest assured that the name of the round matters far less than the quality of your idea, team, etc. Still, no one wants to open the meeting trying to raise a Series A as a first-time founder—especially not one for $250,000.

That's the startup equivalent of having a little spinach in your teeth. We've all been there and many a marriage has begun with that little spot of mouth green, but let's avoid it if we can.

First thing we need to differentiate is who is writing the check versus what the round is called. These are two different things.

Terms like angel round, friends-and-family round, and VC round are describing *what kinds of people are participating*.

Terms like pre-seed, seed, Series A, etc., are describing *a stage progression of rounds*—and you don't need to do all of them. What's even more confusing is that sometimes companies retroactively try to rename the rounds. They'll raise a $3 million seed round with plans to go for a Series A in 12 months only to raise a $5 million seed round at the time, now referring to the previous one as a pre-seed retroactively.

To make things even more complicated, sometimes you need money between rounds. You missed your goals and now you're trying to figure out how you get from where you are to where you need to be to earn another real round.

The one thing everyone in venture seems pretty certain about is that you don't want to call it a bridge. Calling it a bridge is like telling people you're "between jobs."

Everyone knows what's up.

These "rescue" rounds are incredibly hard and are usually done by insiders who still believe—which is yet another reason to keep an active dialogue with your current investors. You never know when you might need to tap them for more support.

A real bridge is reserved when you're actually bridging to something—like a bridge to a near certain sale of a company. A bridge to more fundraising isn't really a bridge.

Hopefully, what you've got is more of an "extension," which is when you're making good progress, but maybe just later than you expected. This is usually priced in the ballpark of the round that its extending—getting investors in on a price that was based on a company with much less progress, so they might see it as a good deal.

How should you keep track to make sure that you're doing all this positioning right? You don't have to! You can take a cue from whoever is participating in the round how to position it. The only think you need to do is be confident about the number.

"What are you raising?"

"We're raising $2 million to get to these big milestones."

"Is this a pre-seed round?"

"It's a $2 million round. Do you think naming it is important? If so, we'd love your input on what to call it *if* you decide to participate."

Anyone who dings you for naming a round "incorrectly" in their mind wasn't too convinced your company was going to return their fund anyway.

If you do want to understand how these things generally work (which is different than saying guidelines—I'm not trying to be prescriptive), here's a typical fundraising path:

"Getting Off the Ground" Rounds
Friends and Family

You might decide that you need a little bit of money to get started. Maybe you want to hire someone to build a super-early version of the product to make a more formal fundraise go more easily or to prove that you can satisfy a customer's need.

Maybe you're trying something technically difficult, and if you get early data that you can pull it off, the rest of the business will be worth pursuing.

You might also be making a decision around social capital. If you feel like you have enough people who would basically write you a check just for being you, regardless of your progress, you might decide just to do that raise first. It might lower your own stress level to get started with a little money in the bank. Plus, if these people are only doing small checks, if they don't get in now, they might not be able to participate—so if you're ever going to call on them, now is the time to do it.

A lot of people call this a friends-and-family round because it usually won't have professionals participating. The size might start around $250,000, because any less than that and it's really hard to build up anything or give yourself much time on that. Given the growth of AI and its affect on software engineering, that might change. For now, I would say if you aren't going to try to pick up at least $250,000 out of the gate, you might be subjecting your friends and family to too much risk, given how little progress you'd be able to make on something smaller.

When you raise a round like this—or any round—I think it's always prudent to make early contact with a set of larger checks for the next round. You might be thinking that you need to build the product first, for example, but perhaps a pre-seed fund that loves your vision is convinced you're not going to be able to build the right product unless you're properly resourced.

Worse comes to worse, they pass, but share their desire to track your progress, and you have a clear sense of what the goals are for the next time you speak to them. The upside is that might tell you not to stop at the $250,000 or $500,000 you're able to raise from your network. They might convince you to go for a proper pre-seed round right away. Your friends-and-family round full of angels suddenly becomes something larger, and you wind up unintentionally starting with pre-seed. That's why many pre-seed rounds have individuals in them—because the founder didn't know how successful they were going to be with real funds, so their earlier commitments were industry folks, people they worked with, or literal family members.

Pre-Seed

These pre-seed rounds, if they contain funds, usually start around $1 million and probably cut off around $3 million or so before someone suggests calling it a seed. The goal of a pre-seed round is usually to get to a commercially viable product that is showing some traction. For consumer applications that traction tends to be more growth oriented than about revenue, and for B2B, sales are key.

How much in sales?

I'd say if you didn't get to at least $20,000 per month in B2B revenues, it's going to be hard to get noticed unless you've got something else special going for you—a proven team, for example.

Seed rounds come in a lot of flavors. There are $3 million seeds and $10 million seeds and everything in between. A $3–5 million seed round probably came after something prior and most of that tally is new money coming in.

As you get larger, there could be a lot of other things going on, including calling it a much larger round because some of those dollars came in via SAFE notes or convertibles and are being converted into this new equity round. So, it's technically a $9 seed round of equity, but only $5 million of that might be new money.

When you're at Series A, you're usually talking about more than $10 million in total funding, but it could be multiples of that. For a Series A, $20 million or more isn't unheard of. When someone pitches me saying that the money they're asking me will lead to a $2 million Series A, it's a bit hard to take seriously. This kind of approach makes it seem like the founder hasn't done the least bit of research on the market, so the only thing I know about him is that he approaches big tasks without being properly prepared.

At the end of the day, the round name is shorthand, not destiny.

Your job isn't to ace a quiz on startup vocabulary—it's to make the case that your company deserves capital. What matters is: Do you know how much you need, what you'll do with it, and why it takes you to the next obvious milestone?

That's the story that gets you funded.

The Pitch to Earn a Pitch

Since I stopped investing, I occasionally do some fundraising consulting workshops with founders.

You can book some time with me here for me to either review a deck and get you my feedback or workshop the full story and approach by scanning this QR Code:

Almost everyone I've worked with thinks we're going to start by opening up the deck and going through the pitch.

That's actually jumping ahead.

You can't get an investor to open the deck unless they like your email first—and that assumes they even read it. They won't read it unless the subject line catches their interest.

That's why the first thing I review is that initial email and its subject.

It's clear that most founders aren't getting this part right. According to DocSend, only about one-third of decks that are sent ever get opened. That makes sense, because investors get thousands of emailed pitchers per year and they have limited time to go through them.

Even if a VC blocked off two hours a day just for new inbound, less than 15% of their week would go to skimming emails. The rest gets swallowed by diligence on the tiny handful of companies that actually pique their interest.

So while a VC might claim they "saw 2,000 companies last year," most of those companies didn't get much of a look.

Which ones do?

The answer: the startups that clearly indicate, in their initial email (not just in the deck), that the company checks at least two boxes out of **market, team, traction.**

- **A great team going after the right market?** That sounds like a partnership meeting worthy investment thesis.
- **A hyper-growth startup that caught fire in a hot space?** Send them a term sheet!
- **A killer team who surprised everyone in a really tough space with exciting revenue growth?** A diamond in the rough.

It's helpful to know which story you are—and just as helpful to understand what we actually mean by "great team," "hyper growth," and "hot space." This way, you can figure out how you're going to highlight it in the short paragraph you have before the links to the deck and in the subject of the email itself. If you can't spell that out clearly upfront, there's no way VCs are going to invest time going through the deck.

Here's what it really means to get the check in each of these areas:

Team. Team. Team.

Every VC will tell you "team is the most important thing."

What they don't say is that "team" doesn't mean what most founders think it does. There are really three categories:

Blank-Check Teams

If you've sold a company before for venture-sized returns, you can raise on day zero. Investors don't need to know what you're working on—they've already seen you turn capital into outcomes. Jack Dorsey didn't need to convince anyone when he started Square after Twitter. Marc Lore raised hundreds of millions for Wonder because he had already sold Jet.com for $3 billion and Diapers.com for $545 million.

Successful founders keep getting backed not because their ideas are always groundbreaking, but because they've proven they can turn capital into outcomes investors care about. The system isn't perfect—biased, insider-driven, and often funding dumb stuff—but it does a decent job of channeling money toward people with a track record of creating big financial wins.

Someone like Marc doesn't raise $50 million pre-product because he's the smartest guy in the room; he raises it because he's sold companies for billions, knows how to avoid first-timer mistakes, and has the network to get things done. Investors don't have to wonder if he'll figure it out—they've already seen him do it. That's the difference between raw potential and demonstrated likelihood of success, and it's why repeat founders keep getting checks while most first-timers struggle.

No-Brainer Meetings

If you didn't have this kind of prior exit, then the best you can hope for is the "great team" category.

VCs think a great team is led by a prior C-level hire for a successful company that built an aspect of the company it was widely known for, or a technical leader at the bleeding edge of research at a top-tier institution.

While maybe not a blank-check team, certainly it would be a "no-brainer meeting" to carve out time for the former VP of Payments at a breakout fintech who scaled its merchant onboarding system to millions of SMBs, the Head of Growth at a consumer app that went from zero to 50 million users in three years, the CTO of a logistics unicorn who built the routing algorithms that became the company's core moat, or a professor at MIT's CSAIL whose lab produced several of the breakthroughs underlying today's foundation models.

They'll also accept someone young and connected, with a kind of "hacker in right circles" pedigree.

That's what the founder of Figma was. Dylan Field didn't have an exit or a C-suite title—he was a Thiel Fellow with Valley credibility, early big-tech internships, and the right network—even getting noticed by Jeff Weiner, CEO of LinkedIn. Jeff was one of the first checks into Figma.

Dylan embodied the plugged-in wunderkind investors love to bet on.

Everyone Else

This is where most founders sit—and it's not bad company. If you're a VP at Chase Bank starting a fintech company, your background is definitely relevant. Just don't expect your title and company to open doors.

Big institutions have thousands of VPs, and it's hard to know if you were a star or just another cog. That's why if you're in this group, you need the other ingredients—traction or a hot market—to tip the scale.

Most founders are in the "everyone else" category—including me if I ever launched something. It's not disqualifying—it just means you need the other ingredients to break through.

Markets Make "meh" Founders Look Like Geniuses

If you're not "that team," being in the right market is the easiest way to get a meeting. Being in the wrong market is also a way to the quickest pass.

If you're playing in an interesting area that investors are looking to write a check into, they're likely to meet with everyone working in that space, if for no other reason than being thorough about their research. That doesn't mean they're going to back you—they just want to make sure that when they do make a bet, they can say they chose the best team and idea out of lots of competition.

What actually makes a great market?

I'll tell you what people get wrong all the time: size.

So many founders will tell me how they're in markets where billions are being spent, but it turns out most of those billions aren't relevant. You can't pitch me hotel software and tell me travel is a trillion-dollar market with half of that being hotels. That money is being spent on hotel rooms, not booking software. If you don't have a bed for someone to sleep in, those aren't relevant dollars for you. Your market is the software used to book that room, which is still a good size, but not in the trillions.

Clothing? Huge market. Most people wear clothes.

Clothing recommendation—tiny market, because most people wouldn't spend much money to be told what to wear.

To make a great market, you need . . .

Tailwinds:

- ✓ A rapidly growing market with tailwinds caused by disruption. Something is changing now—technology costs dropping, regulation changes, generational consumer shifts.
- ✓ You want something that people already spend a lot of money on, but one where they can't just spend it with all the companies they've spent money with before because something has changed and the whole market is up for grabs.

Structure:

- ✓ You don't want a market where someone huge already dominates, but you can't have it be a market where no one's ever gotten big. VCs will start to wonder if it isn't possible.

- ✓ You want real customer pain—not a small annoyance they've lived with for a while and aren't willing to pay to solve.
- ✓ Ideally, you'd want a market structure that lends itself to network effects, where the more customers you get the bigger your moat will be.

Economics:

- ✓ Repeatable demand where there's recurring usage of a product and it's not a one-time or one-off purchase.
- ✓ The ability to generate high margins. SaaS-like businesses with 70–90% margins or marketplaces with strong take-rates are more investable than thin-margin services.

Ability to scale:

- ✓ Ability to scale distribution: The market allows viral growth, low CAC channels, or piggybacking on existing platforms.
- ✓ Data flywheels: Unique datasets that accumulate over time, improving product and defensibility.
- ✓ Ecosystem leverage: A market where building one layer lets you expand into others.

While there are "unsexy" markets that some VCs get excited about as a thesis, usually great markets have innovation happening in them. That doesn't mean a startup that sounds exactly like yours has been funded and we should think that's "validating"—but you at least want to see *some* movement to build things by interesting founders backed by experienced investors.

Market and team are things that an investor feel like an expert in analyzing. They can tell you what makes the teams they back great and the markets they go into lucrative.

To the Moon!

Traction, on the other hand, is the great equalizer. This is the lever you can pull where you're the one going in and telling the investor that what you have is working and, at certain levels of growth, they're not going to be able to argue with it.

Traction can excuse a team that hasn't accomplished much of anything before and, if you're making money, defeats the "terrible market" label.

How much traction is enough is something founders want to know and, unfortunately, investors hate to answer with specifics.

I'll tell you what the right amount of traction feels like:

Real traction doesn't feel like a slog. It feels like the market is pulling your product out of your hands as fast as you can tell people about it. They're not just "excited about it," they're paying for it. They're also paying more and more for it each month, because they're expanding usage, paying for new features, etc.

Customers also don't need long explanations or persuasion—they hear what you do and immediately see the value. Instead of chasing down every lead, you start getting inbounds, referrals, or waitlist signups. Customers might even abandon existing contracts to move over. There's a rhythm forming, a repeatable playbook that works beyond the first lucky customer.

Also, if you extrapolate out the current traction, the numbers will lead to somewhere big and venture-sized without a suspension of reality. An investor can take a look at the numbers you're doing as the company's only salesperson, spending only 30% of your time on it, and they're excited to imagine what an experienced, full-time sales hire could do.

VCs want to make fast judgments with limited information. It's a bit like arguing whether someone is worthy to be enshrined in the Baseball Hall of Fame.

If you have to debate whether your traction is impressive enough, it probably isn't.

So before you obsess over kerning in the deck, focus on the 30 seconds that really matter—the email. Make your subject line irresistible, then use the body to check at least two boxes: team, market, or traction. Spell out the win in plain English, don't bury it. If you can show "this is the 'must meet' team, in the market with lots of cash sloshing around it, already moving forward," you'll get the click.

Miss that, and the deck never even has a chance.

An Idea Is Like a Virus

Everything you need to know about pitching you can learn from the movie *Inception*—the Leonardo DiCaprio movie about shared dreaming and breaking into someone else's unconscious.

In *Inception*, DiCaprio's character, Cobb, is a professional thief who steals information by infiltrating the subconscious. He is offered a chance to have his criminal history erased as payment for a seemingly impossible task: "inception," the implantation of another person's idea into a target's subconscious.

Just like Cobb planting an idea in his target's head, your job isn't to transfer your vision wholesale, but to design a narrative so convincing the investor feels like they dreamt it up themselves.

A pitch deck's job is to implant a simple, emotional, self-generated belief in the investor's mind about your future potential.

When it works, they'll start pitching it back to you in the meeting.

As Tom Hardy's *Inception* character states, "It's a very subtle art" that requires creativity.

Many founders, on the other hand, build decks that are technically correct but uninspiring: bullet points, TAM numbers, and product screenshots. They ask their network for templates and try to copy "The Pitch Deck That Got Plaid Its Seed Round" from LinkedIn.

Never mind that Plaid raised a seed round in 2013 at a time before ... well ... Plaid. Plaid's deck isn't going to work once someone has built Plaid.

Your story has to be built for this moment, and for this investor—because their defenses are trained to say no.

For it to grow naturally in their mind, like a seed, the idea needs to be simple, uncomplicated. If it takes 20 pages of a deck for someone to be convinced, it will feel like something unwieldy is being pushed on them. It will meet with mental resistance.

The Hook

The right seed makes them light up from the very first description. It will generate emotion. The rest of the information just cements its place in the investor's mind to make sure it sticks.

Julian Shapiro, a prolific writer, founder, and startup investor has a guide to writing good nonfiction. Consider it a cheat sheet for planting ideas.

"A novel idea is one that's not just new to the reader, but also significant and not easily intuited. Think of it as new and worthwhile. I've identified five categories:

- *Counter-intuitive—"Oh, I never realized the world worked that way."*
- *Counter-narrative—"Wow, that's not how I was told the world worked!"*
- *Shock and awe—"That's crazy. I would have never believed it."*
- *Elegant articulations—"Beautiful. I couldn't have said it better myself."*
- *Make someone feel seen—"Yes! That's exactly how I feel!"*

Novelty is what gives readers dopamine hits. You find novel ideas by pursuing your curiosity and noting what interests and surprises you along the way. If it intrigues you, it'll likely intrigue your readers too."

This is a super helpful way to think about this seed and its initial "hook."

You can lose an investor in the first 30 seconds if you open the wrong way. The fastest way to shut down curiosity is to lead with the wrong part of your story.

A founder came up to me at an event and launched straight in:

"I'm building a new social network."

She rattled off a flurry of features I don't remember—because she lost me at "new social network."

Remember, I was just a career VC—a lower-order Neanderthal cave person. I pick up random objects, sniff them, bang them against the wall and the floor saying, "Money? Money? Is this money?"

Most things a cave person picks up aren't money, obviously.

The same goes for startups. Most of them won't turn into money—so the moment you lose someone in a flurry of details that don't sound lucrative, you'll get a grunt from your prominently browed investor:

"Ug-ha. Not money."

And they're probably right, because being a VC is so easy, even a cave person can do it.

This founder lost me on her pitch not because I think the world doesn't need a new social network. I'm pretty tired of what's out there and so are a lot of other people.

It's not because lots of money hasn't been made in new social networks—it clearly has.

When you open with a product description, the investor invents the product in their head before you can even describe it. You say you're building a time machine and they're mentally picturing the

DeLorean from *Back to the Future* in your garage before you can open your pitch deck.

If they're skeptical about the space, they'll picture the worst version of whatever you're building. If they're optimistic, they'll picture the perfect version—only to be let down that your thing doesn't do everything they were hoping for.

Here's how I recommended that she flip her pitch to avoid getting shot down before she had a chance to really get into her pitch:

Get them to want to talk to you about the problem, not the product.

Convince them that it will be an interesting chat about an area that has vexed founders, investors, and consumers alike—one that will help push their thinking on what the ultimately successful solution will look like in the space. That's an easier thing to convince someone of than getting them to assume you built the next big thing based on the first 30 seconds of your pitch.

Investors talk to a lot of people that they don't ultimately wind up investing in—not just because most ideas aren't very good. A good investor spends a lot of time learning. They're investing in new areas that are changing every day, so talking to people who aren't ready to pitch yet, or who don't have anything to pitch, is a teaching moment.

That means you can increase your chances of getting a meeting if you can just convince someone you're working on a worthwhile problem, while downplaying the specifics of whether or not you have the right idea. Maybe you do, maybe you don't, but when you convince someone that you're smart and the problem you're addressing is huge, people will want to chat just to learn.

Maybe you can figure out the answers together, or maybe you'll knock their socks off with your idea. Either way, you're just trying to get the full pitch meeting. You can increase your chances of getting one by checking the box of being a smart person also exploring a space they're interested in.

I suggested that she open with the statement "Gen Z hates LinkedIn, but they still have professional goals and aspirations. They're open to achieving those somewhere else and I have some insights as to what they'll need from those spaces and how to get them to join."

LinkedIn is obviously a very large, successful company—but if there's a whole younger generation that seems unlikely to use it, maybe there is, in fact, some white space in the social networking market.

Investors, who probably aren't Gen Z themselves, would be highly likely to shoot the shit about what a Gen Z professional networking platform might look like—as long as it's with someone who knows what they're talking about. They'd want to understand how Gen Z networks differently online than their Millennial or Gen X counterparts.

The next step is convincing someone that you're legit—that your insights and ideas are going to be interesting and unique before you get a chance to share them.

You can do this in two ways:

First is to drop a really good teaser hook—a surprising data point they're going to be intrigued by and that will show them that you're well informed and have done lots of homework.

What stat would make someone go: "Wait, really?"

Here are some good ones:

> "About 30% of 18–24-year-olds have no credit . . . not bad credit, but just no credit data and therefore have no credit score. They did a great job avoiding the pitfalls of credit card abuse—so they're super responsible—but yet no one wants to lend to them because all lending is based on credit scores."
>
> "Ninety-six percent of baby food on grocery shelves is older than your baby—sometimes over a year old."
>
> "HR and IT teams spend 80+ hours manually onboarding each new hire."

What I love each of these is that they don't pitch a product, they pitch a problem. When someone says, "That's ridiculous, how is it still that bad?" then you've got them open to hearing about a solution.

Plus, anyone would agree with these being real problems—and, the severity of the issue would be really surprising to most.

Thirty percent of college age kids won't have the credit history to ever get a car loan or a mortgage—that's an issue!

We're feeding babies old food? Who's going to argue that's not an issue?

Eighty hours *per hire*?? That's nuts!

Too often, however, is that founders open with things that sound like issues but really aren't.

"In the United States, K–12 schools spend less than 3% of their budget on digital tools, despite 90% of kids using screens daily."

Well, that's a disconnect, but, a lot of people think that kids use screens too much. Plus, the math isn't mathing—90% of kids using screens once a day doesn't mean that 90% of our education budget should be digital.

"The average traveler spends over 10 hours across 20+ websites planning a single trip."

I know you're presenting this a problem, and I get it because I hate trip planning, but my wife would present this as a fun thing to do on a weekend.

Pitches that promise centralization and efficiency often overlook what some people see as the value in something—the journey itself and "the friends we made along the way." Sometimes friction isn't so bad. Using different websites for different things can allow you to have best-of-breed solutions for specific aspects of a problem. Having middlemen might ultimately increase sales if the customer needs to be handheld—or they might serve as some kind of filtering mechanism.

Higgs Bono

Another way to pique someone's interest is to have a "mic drop" founder or team bio. Once I had dinner with a guy who was on the team that discovered the Higgs Boson—one of the 17 fundamental particles of the universe.

I barely have a clue what the 17 fundamental particles of the universe are, but that's not going to stop me from being an automatic yes to that invite.

When I was on the institutional investment side at the General Motors pension fund, I once took a meeting with a fund that included several prominent investors and tech executives—and Paul David Hewson.

You might know him as Bono.

We didn't look at the deck before the meeting—because Bono. Who wouldn't want to meet with Bono for an hour?

To answer your most important questions—yes, he kept the Dolce & Gabbana sunglasses on the whole time, indoors. He wore a jacket and collared shirt, but no tie. And he's small . . . really small. I doubt he's even the 5'6" that he's listed as—but he was still the biggest person in the room, because he's Bono. He was also incredibly thoughtful about the industry and fascinating to speak with. If you know Bono, please feel free to tell him how impressed I was with him in that meeting 20+ years ago and I'll pretend he cares.

Do you have a Bono on your team? Are you the Bono of vertical SaaS applications?

You might not be Bono, but you'll get a meeting if someone is clear they could learn from you in a space they care about—the kind of person who, if that investor has future startups they're vetting, you might be the person they go to for due diligence.

Investors don't fund features. They fund curiosity, credibility, and conviction. So before you try to sell your time machine, make sure you've convinced someone there's a reason to build it—and that you're the person who can.

Give Me Two Good Reasons

Start with your "two out of three" category: Team + Market, Market + Traction, or Team + Traction.

What can you say about those two big checkmarks that will generate a dopamine hit?

Will someone be excited to meet and speak with your team?

Are they stunned at the size of a big market they didn't realize existed?

Will they be in utter disbelief about how fast you are moving?

(If these all feel like a stretch, you have to go back to the drawing board and figure out the barriers to these things being big yeses.)

The Game of VC Partner Meeting Telephone

The other reason why your hook needs to both create excitement and be simple is because of how VC firms work internally. Whoever you pitch to is going to have to create internal momentum if you're ever going to get a check.

On Monday morning, they're going to meet as a group and tell each other what they've seen in the past week. It's a blur of ideas seeking early team support. Without it, an investor is going to feel like they're pushing a rock up a hill.

Here's what it must accomplish to survive the whole team's subconscious defenses.

It Has to Be Idiot-Proof

They're going to botch your pitch in the worst way, because you're not the one delivering it. You don't want it to devolve into, "I met a guy, doing this thing . . . I dunno, it's like . . . they put a chip in a cow, and then, there's some data, and somehow, investors participate. . . I dunno."

That's not going to win anyone over.

It Can't Be Easily Dismissed

One partner saying, "That's never going to work for X reason," is enough to kill all the momentum on a deal.

It Has to Feel Big

Everyone's looking for the next big fund returner and unless you find a way to convince people that your Pog trading site will unlock an eBay killer, no one's going to get psyched.

This last part—the bigness—needs to be pervasive. Every single page in your deck needs to support the argument that they're going to make a ton of money on this. Too many slides in a row that don't show this—especially upfront—and you've lost their attention.

Go with the Flow

In fact, any individual slide in a deck is easily forgotten. That's why it's got to flow as a cohesive story—not just a series of slides that fit a structure you saw online somewhere. Stories are memory hacks. Just like retracing your steps in a dream to remember how you got to a strange café, a narrative helps investors recall the facts.

That's why building a deck should never start in PowerPoint, Canva, or any other program that allows you to put pen to paper right on the presentation itself. You should be starting with a short set of bullets, but here's what not to do:

- Team
- Product
- Market

- Features
- Traction
- Financials
- Competition

That's just structure. It's not narrative. It doesn't flow.

The bullets need to *say something*. Here's what each of these slides could say:

- We're an amazing team.
- Here's what we built.
- This is a huge market opportunity.
- This is how clever we were about what we built and why it's working.
- Look at how quickly we're growing.
- With some money, we can get HUGE.
- We're lightyears ahead of everyone else.

Yet, this still seems like bad flow.

Founders should read their own deck and imagine what is going through a VC's head as they read or listen. While you might hope for the kind of warm and fuzzy support that your mom, beaming with pride, might give you, who you're actually getting is something more akin to Simon Cowell.

In fact, try this ChatGPT prompt on for size after uploading your deck:

> *"Imagine I'm a real pompous ass of a VC . . . not a bad person, but just someone who has backed some serious winners and feels like they've seen it all. The "Simon Cowell" of VCs. What's your internal monologue after each of these slides?"*

Are you horrified by the results? Good. Now we know how to make it Simon-proof.

Take each slide and consider whether I've seen anything exciting yet and what my next question is going to be. What are the most obvious ways I can be dismissive? Does this slide really need to be here if it doesn't strengthen your case?

Here's what Simon Cowell the VC might be saying to our deck from above:

- We're an amazing team. *Okay, but I wouldn't write a blank check to this team. Not sold yet.*
- Here's what we built. *I'm not the customer, so I don't know if this is good or not.*
- This is a huge market opportunity. *Ah, okay, I guess that's good . . .*
- This is how clever we were about what we built and why it's working. *So you say.*
- Look at how quickly we're growing. *Okay, but I kinda checked out already because most of the previous slides were meh.*
- With some money, we can get HUGE. *Cool, I'm kinda back now.*

What if we flipped around the order to maintain the momentum from the beginning?

- Look at how quickly we're growing. *You have my attention and now I wonder what this is.*
- This is how clever we were about what we built and why it's working. *Interesting!*
- With some money, we can get HUGE. *Wow. Okay, but is this a big enough market?*
- This is a huge market opportunity. *Fuck yeah! But wait, too good to be true. Who else is doing this?*

- We're lightyears ahead of everyone else. *Weeeeeeeeeeeeeeeeee!*
- We're an amazing team. *Sure, fine, whatever . . . I'm sure you'll need to learn more and hire people . . . but let's introduce you to my partners!*
- ~~Here's what we built.~~ *I'm so glad you didn't show me a feature walkthrough because that bores the hell out of me. No one likes watching someone else use something and I'm not the customer anyway.*

One other thing—something I've probably repeated to founders more than any other piece of advice—is that investors aren't rewarding you for the past by investing. At least 80% of your pitch story should be about *what's next*, not what you've done previously.

This isn't a scrapbook of what you've done. It's a trailer for the blockbuster that hasn't been made yet. If investors can picture themselves in the credits, they'll fight to buy a ticket.

Write three bullets that would make an investor say "holy shit" about your team, traction, or market. Test them in your pre-board.

Do they retell it back to you simply and with excitement?

Build your deck around those bullets, not the template.

What You're Up Against in the Meeting

Here's what's true of just about every sit down with an investor:

1. They're distracted—another deal, a portfolio fire, the market, family drama, or just a bad lunch.
2. They're hoping you can be the next big thing, but they're going to be super quick to lose that hope if you haven't worked hard to maintain it in every possible moment.

3. They're half paying attention to your words and half trying to figure you out—your motivations, strengths, weaknesses, and whether your go-to bagel order is disqualifying. (Maybe this is a NYC investor thing.)
4. They bring their unconscious bias into the room with them, as do you, assuming all sorts of things about who you are because they've been socialized that way.
5. They're trying to associate you with other better-known companies to help understand what you've built.

Investors walk in distracted and biased. Your job is to win their attention back.

Here's how:

- Capturing their attention with high energy and constant engagement.
- Making sure that every statement lands—and lands big.
- Getting ahead of all the potential objections, especially the ones someone might have about you personally.
- Creating a framework for them to understand your business anchored by successful precedent.

Let's dive deeper into how to do all this.

First off, you're not reading the deck. This is where a lot of founders mess up. They create decks that are meant to be read and then they try to read them in person when meeting investors. The fact is that an investor can read three times faster than you can speak.

While my toddler loves when Daddy reads to her, investors will be much less enthusiastic.

The truth is you're dealing with two different tools that get unfairly mashed together:

- The **"read deck"** is designed to standalone. It's dense. It has enough sentences, context, and data that someone who's never met you can make sense of the story.
- The **"presentation deck"** is designed for the room. Big headlines, simple visuals, minimal text. The founder provides the story, the pacing, the punchlines.

Trying to do both in one usually fails. The read deck gets boring in person, and the presentation deck confuses anyone who opens it without you there.

How to Fix It

1. **Make two versions.** Send the "read deck" in advance. Present from the "presentation deck." Don't overcomplicate this. Copy and paste the slides, trim down the text, and treat it like two deliverables.
2. **Control the flow.** If you only want them to focus on what you're saying, screen-share instead of sending the file before the meeting. Or set expectations: "I'll send you a detailed version, but live I'll walk you through the highlights." That way you're not competing with their reading speed.
3. **Design for dual use.** If you can't stomach making two files, at least separate them within one. Keep the main slides light and conversational, then load the appendix or notes section with detail for when the deck gets forwarded around.
4. **Narrate what they can't read.** Don't repeat the words on the screen. Talk about context, why it matters, what's surprising,

what the data doesn't show. Investors read fast, but they don't automatically know what's important. That's your role.

Remember the Purpose

A deck is not the performance. You are. The slides are props. They keep the conversation structured, but the real persuasion happens in the back-and-forth, not in the bullet points. If they read ahead, let them. Your job is to keep pulling them back to the meaning of the story, not the words on the page.

Now that you've got the right deck backup singing for you, start your pitch with confidence and energy. Your presence should make investors sit up. No mumbling.

Let them feel your conviction, no matter how many hours of sleep you got the night before. Look them right in the eye. There's no reason for you to look at the deck because you know which slide comes next and what's on it.

Qualify the room. Make sure everyone in there is excited to be there for the right reason by getting buy-in on your core belief.

See if the investor agrees.

> *"I'm here because I think cost effectively turning any kind of garbage into construction bricks that last forever would be an enormous financial opportunity. Do you agree?"*
>
> *"I think that LinkedIn was built for people who have long-term jobs, not a portfolio of projects—and Gen Z is going to be open to a new, more creative, collaborative professional platform. Do you know of any Gen Zers excited about LinkedIn? If not, let's talk more about what we're building and why."*

These Are Not the Droids You're Looking For

If they don't say yes to that, thank them for their time and move on. If they do, they're bought into the meeting from the beginning and are now more mentally "open" to what you have to say.

From then on you want to make sure that what you're saying gets more and more engagement along the way. Drop anything that kills the flow or that feels lazy.

This includes:

X for Y (Unless You Nailed It)

"Uber for pediatricians" sounds clever but misses the stakes. Parents expect far more rigor from a doctor than a driver, so the analogy cheapens trust. If you must use X-for-Y, pick comparisons where the stakes and dynamics actually match—and only use a company that is recently, but clearly successful with an exit or hundreds of millions in revenue.

The TAM Slide

Everyone has a big number here. Everyone overestimates how much of that is actually addressable. Just because you're in the travel space doesn't mean I can swap my hotel budget to spend more money on your recommendation app. Show how your first beachhead nets $100–200 million in realistic annual revenue over time. Once investors see a credible wedge, they can dream forward to the big number themselves.

Features and Demos

Is your demo magical? If you're building a B2B SaaS tool, I'd assume not. No one needs to be shown how you sign in to the app. Ever watch your parents try to use the internet? This is how it feels when a founder drives a demo for a VC. Unless you're doing something literally amazing, don't show it. Let your traction do the talking. If you don't have traction, ask the VC for a recommendation to talk to a potential customer. Let the customer come back and rave about what they saw for you.

Problems That Aren't Problems

Finding everything "all in one place" doesn't really solve that much of a problem if I can do the work pretty quickly with two or three browser tabs open. That's certainly never been a big enough moat to IPO. Anchor your problem to real pain: money lost, compliance risk, jail time, locusts!

Testimonials

If they're not in the investor's inbox from people they know, they're not going to count. You could have made them up—and all together they probably amount to $200 in monthly revenue from consumers. If they're from a million-dollar enterprise client, that's a different story. That's case study worthy.

Competitive Landscapes

Four quadrants with an arbitrary axis like "easy to use" versus "hard to use," which no one has ever objectively measured. Of course, you put the $2 billion a year in sales competitor all the way on the hard to use side. This tells me that either it's not as hard to use as you think or maybe it doesn't matter. The axis is always something like, "Bad for people who are terrible customers with no money to pay for this thing" versus "Only works for big, deep-pocket enterprises that have huge problems and spend a lot of money." Obviously, you haven't written it out this way, but that's often the way it looks to an investor.

Show why customers switch to you despite incumbents. Actual replacement stories beat invented axes.

The Five Ds of a Pitch Meeting: Dodge. Duck. Dip. Dive. Dodge.

Founders often walk into investor meetings thinking their job is to survive scrutiny—to answer whatever comes their way as precisely as possible, almost like an oral exam.

That's a trap.

If you spend the entire meeting reacting to the wrong questions, you miss your chance to tell the story that actually gets someone excited.

There's hard data on this. A study published in *Harvard Business Review* found that male founders are disproportionately asked promotion-oriented questions about growth, scale, and upside, while women are disproportionately asked prevention-oriented questions about risk, competition, or downside. The consequences are massive: in the data set, founders who were mostly asked promotion questions went on to raise roughly seven times more capital than those who faced mostly prevention questions. Every single prevention-oriented question correlated with millions of dollars less in funding.

So, if you're a woman founder—or anyone who keeps getting pulled into a defensive frame—you have to understand what's really happening. The investor isn't just asking questions; they're shaping the terms of the conversation. And if you let them control the frame, you'll find yourself playing not to lose, instead of playing to win.

The way out is the same technique that great politicians use: acknowledge the question, then pivot back to what matters most—your vision, your traction, and your path to big outcomes. You're not dodging. You're redirecting to the conversation that needs to happen if the investor is going to get excited about your company.

For example, if someone asks, "How will you avoid losing customers?," you don't have to spend the next five minutes defending churn.

Acknowledge that you understand the issue, but stress that your strength is everything that you're doing to prevent it: "Churn can kill a business if you're not addressing customer needs. The reason why someone would churn out is because of X, Y, and Z. Those three things are exactly why we built this. They're the reasons why our customers are joining us from other platforms. We wouldn't built this if it wasn't to fix those very issues."

"That's also why we're growing so much, because our customers are telling everyone else who still uses their prior platform to come to us. We've grown X% month over month, and here's the strategy that triples our user base over the next year."

That's not evasion—it's discipline.

It's making sure the meeting is about why your company could be big, not why it might fail. The goal isn't to just survive a grilling. It's to create clarity, enthusiasm, and momentum—on your terms.

You Hear This Pitch? It's the Sound of Inevitability

Startup success is never simple. It takes relentless effort from founders and early employees. You need people who can move fast, make smart decisions, and avoid major mistakes. Even then, it's brutally hard to gain traction.

Unless the market pulls you forward.

Nail the timing, and even a decent team with a passable product can ride a wave they didn't create.

Of course, you don't often hear people describe it that way. No one likes to admit they just opened the doors at the right moment and were more lucky than good.

What do you hear all the time? "We were too early." People will say that they had the best team and a killer product, but the market wasn't ready.

If being too early can sink a great team and a killer product, doesn't that mean the inverse is also true? Wouldn't great timing supercharge a decent team and an okay product?

You wouldn't pitch your startup that way—but you can harness the same force by showing investors the trend first. Hook them on the market momentum before you even explain why you or your product win.

A few years ago, Drew Lederman pitched me Resist, her nutrition bar company. She and her co-founder Emily Cohen had a compelling personal story—solving their own health challenges by creating a bar that wouldn't spike blood sugar or mess with hormones.

I'll be honest—my caveman VC brain went: "Too many bars. Move on."

That reflex wasn't wrong. It is crowded space.

Still, some bars break out—Kind ($5 billion), Clif ($3 billion), Quest ($1 billion), RxBar ($600 million).

Timing and trend fit explain a lot of their success.

What I suggested to Drew and Emily was that they didn't need to convince investors this was the best bar ever made. They just had to make a simple, plausible case: Every time there's a new nutrition trend, a bar wins. Clean-ingredient, hormone-friendly is next wave.

We're early—but not too early.

That framing made the opportunity feel *plausible*.

This thing has happened before, so it's possible that it *could* happen again.

Bill Magnuson, the co-founder and CEO of Braze, echoed the same sentiment. Long before his company IPO'd and became worth billions of dollars, it was a tiny startup struggling to find product-market fit. It was a bit too early to its category, but the team was confident the market would come around—even if their traction didn't indicate that it was a winner.

Rather than try to convince skeptical generalists, Bill focused on finding investors who had seen this movie before—people who had backed marketing platforms or developer tools in previous cycles and made "some" money doing it (but not billions).

These weren't investors who needed to be educated on the space; they already understood the dynamics, timing, and potential upside. Bill's pitch wasn't "Here's why this could work"—it was "You know this story. We're running it back, but this time with a bigger market, a stronger team, and better timing."

That pattern-matching gave investors a frame of reference and made it easier for them to believe.

That's the trick—give people something familiar to latch onto. If you have to teach an investor everything from scratch—the problem, the product, the customer—it's a long climb. But if they already believe in the wave you're riding, everything else becomes easier to believe too.

That's why "X for Y" analogies work. VCs don't hate them because they're lazy—they just hate the bad ones.

The right one creates instant clarity.

Chewy.com: Amazon for pet supplies—Acquired by PetSmart for $3.35 billion, IPO'd later at $8.7 billion.

StockX: NASDAQ for sneakers—Valued at $3.8 billion as of 2021.

These examples gave investors a language and infrastructure they already understood.

It's just easier to get excited when it doesn't take 30 minutes of granular explanation to get something—from the inner workings of your product to the market dynamics that are going to catapult you into success.

Chapter 10

Dogs and Cats, Living Together

Mass Hysteria! Getting Yeses and Nos

One of the most dangerous words a founder can hear from an investor is "interested." It sounds positive—but it usually means nothing.

The danger is that founders mistake "interested" for progress. They think it's one step closer to a check, when in reality, it's the investor's default state—a polite holding pattern.

When Interested Is a No

Investors are, by definition, always *interested*. They're curious about what's happening in the market, they want to keep tabs on smart founders, and they're open to being surprised. Plus, they know that founders often wander in the wilderness a bit before figuring something out.

- **Twitter started as a podcasting platform called Odeo.** When Apple announced iTunes would include podcasts, Odeo was dead in the water. The team pivoted to a side project Jack Dorsey had been noodling on—microblogging via SMS.
- **Slack started as a multiplayer online game called Glitch.** The game shut down, but the internal chat tool the team built to collaborate remotely became the real product.

- **Shopify was originally an online snowboard shop called Snowdevil.** The founders couldn't find good e-commerce software, so they built their own—and realized that was the real opportunity.

Imagine meeting these founders for their original idea and saying, *"Welp. That was your one shot. Don't come back to pitch me for any reason, including pivoting into a completely different idea based on market pull."* You would look terrible for letting those teams walk out the door—so you find ways of keeping it just a little bit open.

Unless you are completely uninvestable, they'll rarely say "not interested."

That's reserved for telemarketers.

So, when you hear "we'd be interested in investing," what they really mean is *"we would, if* you became exactly the kind of company we already want to invest in."

In other words: we're not there . . . forget "yet."

They're not there.

How to Turn Interested into a Yes

It's your job to figure out if they can get there and push past "interested" into specifics:

- What's blocking you from a yes?
- What conviction do you need to get there?
- Who else on your team needs to be won over?
- Why did you even take this meeting?

If you don't ask those questions, you risk building a pipeline full of polite maybes that never convert.

Remember: until you hear yes, every investor is a no. This can be tricky because you'll hear the word "interested" paired with a bunch of phrases that feel like they want to make an investment:

- **What they say:** "We'd be interested in putting in $500,000."
- **Translation:** "If we actually liked the company, this is what we'd do. We're just telling you what our normal check size is in case you talk to a more interesting company and they wanna know."
- **What you really need**: "We're 'in' for $500,000 on these terms. Please send us the docs."

Just because they talk about how they invest doesn't mean this is how they'd like to invest in you. The same goes for when they discuss how they lead deals.

What they say: "We'd be interested in leading."

Translation: "I see your round is almost done. We're looking for a way to politely decline, so we're telling you that if we were going to do this, you'd have to be willing to upend the whole thing for us, which we assume/hope you won't be willing to do."

What you really need: "Here's a term sheet."

If they're not willing to lead, you might hear them take out some schmuck insurance. (An expression I learned from Josh Kopelman of First Round Capital. It basically means they're looking for a way to cover their butts if it turns out one of the top VC firms in the world wants in on this deal after they pass.)

What they say: "If you got a strong lead, we'd be interested in joining a round."

Translation: "We don't think there's anything here, but if Benchmark comes in, maybe we missed something and we'd be happy to come in alongside them."

What you really need: "We're 'in' for $500,000 on these terms. Please send us the docs."

What Leading Really Means

Founders often get whiplash when an investor says, "We don't lead." That phrase sounds definitive, but it's vague enough to mean a dozen different things.

Do they mean they won't set the valuation? Fine, the company can set it at a reasonable number no one will balk at.

They won't negotiate documents? What if one of the smaller but still sophisticated checks will? Maybe they want to be seen as stepping up and leading.

They won't take a board seat for bandwidth issues? Fine, let's hire a strong independent or maybe find someone they know and they're comfortable with to join.

Or do they just mean they want to see someone else go first so they don't feel like the only one writing a check? That can't really be helped.

You can't take "we don't lead" at face value.

Be direct and ask what they actually mean when they say it. Sometimes, what they're unwilling to do is only one piece of the puzzle, and you can still work with them if you can cover the rest. Maybe they won't negotiate the docs, but they'll happily be the biggest check. Maybe they won't price the round, but they'll introduce you to firms that will.

The key is to break down what "lead" really requires:

- Setting terms
- Negotiating documents
- Putting in a meaningful check size
- Taking governance responsibility (like a board seat)
- Signaling to others that they've diligenced you

Once you separate those out, you can figure out if you actually need a traditional lead, or if you can assemble those functions across different investors. In some cases, a "no-lead" round can work fine, as long as someone is stepping up on the major points that give other investors confidence. What doesn't work is assuming "we don't lead" is a dead end. Push for clarity, then decide whether you can still close without them—or whether you should move on.

Fund or Get Off the Pot

You might be thinking, "Okay, so they didn't say all of these things, but this one investor at a firm is spending *a lot* of time with me. They wouldn't keep meeting if they weren't *really* interested, right?"

Plus, I already met one of the partners!

This is a classic "gone rogue" investor. Usually, it happens when a junior person at a firm (which is sometimes hard to tell now that everyone has a partner title) meets a company they actually really like. They do a bunch of work on it and present it to a partner, who agrees to take a meeting.

Rather than say no, they meet with you for the same optionality reason it's difficult to get a VC to say no directly to a founder. You don't want to be the partner who turned down the next big thing, so you sandbag the deal with questions—specifically, the kind of questions that are difficult to answer definitively.

"How do these guys get big?"

"Is this team really able to scale a company?"

"How defensible is this?"

After your meeting where the original sourcer brought in a partner, they've come back with all sorts of questions.

Do you know what they didn't come back with? A term sheet or a commitment to invest.

Now you're busy answering all these random questions over two more meetings, thinking the firm is really engaging. Meanwhile, the partner you met with wouldn't even remember the company name if he heard it.

There's a path for these things to move forward in a firm. It involves meeting more and more of the team each time, with multiple members showing engagement. If you're not getting that, you're on an analyst's due diligence treadmill going nowhere.

The bottom line: "interested" is not a commitment, it's camouflage.

It keeps founders hopeful while giving investors all the optionality to see the next card turned over—and they've got zero incentive to turn that information flow off.

When It's a Real Yes

Let's say you get a yes.

What do you actually do with it?

That all depends on few factors—the first being whether you're raising equity or on another type of security like a note, or more commonly these days, a SAFE.

Most of the money in an equity round needs to be pulled together in a single close. Fundraising is expensive in more ways than one. Every close means another round of legal documents, wires, board consents, and cap table updates. If you're dragging your round out across a series of mini-closes, you're repeating that whole process again and again. It eats up time, adds costs, and creates room for mistakes. You don't want to be managing your law firm's billing hours when you should be managing your company. Pulling most of the money together in a single close keeps the paperwork clean and lets you get back to building.

It also generally leads a lead—a single counterpart to negotiate the documents with. A lead centralizes that process. They hammer out the terms once, you lock them in, and everyone else joins under the same structure. Without a lead, you're stuck negotiating 10 different times. With a lead, you negotiate once.

The small guys are now allowed to change the terms of a big lead and they shouldn't waste your legal fees to attempt it.

Having a lead also strengthens your story. Instead of saying, "We're still piecing the round together," you can point to a credible investor who has already diligenced the company, signed off on the terms, and is putting meaningful capital behind you. That social proof helps herd the rest of the round into place and makes it harder for latecomers to second-guess the structure. In other words: one negotiation, one set of documents, one anchor investor—much cleaner, much faster, and far more compelling to everyone else.

A SAFE, or note, on the other hand, doesn't require all the money to come in at once—but it can certainly have a lead as well. It doesn't have to. These are lighter-weight agreements, meant to be simple and fast, and they don't trigger all the legal and administrative overhead of a priced equity round. You can let checks roll in over time without having to amend your cap table every week. That's why early-stage founders often use SAFEs or convertible notes for smaller, less formal raises—they're designed for flexibility. Just be mindful that the convenience can cut both ways: the longer you leave the door open, the more you risk confusing your own fundraising story or creating mismatched expectations with investors.

That being said, it's actually pretty stupid for an investor to put money into a round before everyone has committed. You at least want the founder to put out some kind of minimum threshold for accomplishing some meaningful goals.

"We'd like to open four more locations this year, but at minimum, $1 million gets us two, which means enough size to breakeven."

"If we only closed $500,000, we'd be able to finish the product and get our first customer. We'd like to raise more to show revenue growth, but we'd be in a good spot just breaking through to revenues."

Yet, for some reason angel investors in particular seem willing to write checks to get the docs off their plate before enough money is in the bank to get them anywhere. I think you have to decide how you want to handle this and whether you feel like it's ethical to close on less than viable amounts and actually accept the money. Certainly I think you have to be upfront about what each amount of money gets you.

Closing on less than a viable amount doesn't just shortchange investors—it puts you in a worse position as a founder, because you'll be under pressure to hit milestones without enough gas in the tank.

Don't Count the Money Until...

Once you decide that minimum threshold, here's how you actually get it in the bank:

1. Once someone says yes, you send them the docs to sign, using Docusign or some other electronic system. Share wire instructions quickly. Tell them (or bake it into the docs) they can wire the money when you hit the round minimum, but you want them signing as soon as they decide the yes.

2. Communicate who is closing, why they're writing the check, and how that person is going to be able to be strategically helpful. I wouldn't tell people when you expect the round to be done, because if that deadline comes and goes, you'll look like you're treading water if you're still raising after it. I would just show the momentum.

3. "Soft commits" don't pay the bills. Track who has signed, who hasn't, and who owes you wires. Don't be afraid to politely nudge—investors are busy, and a little persistence is often the difference between verbal and actual dollars. Follow up with anyone who said yes at least every 48 hours if you need a signature from them.

4. If someone ghosts you, invite them to a calendar meeting. Email or text them saying that you've done so and expect them to be on the call to discuss finalizing the close, but to let you know if that time doesn't work for them. Obnoxious? Maybe, but how you herd the cats in a fundraising round is a signal for how you bring enterprise customers and other partners on board. If someone feels like you're incredibly on top of things and they can't shake you, they'll feel more confident about you than they feel harassed by you. Besides, they said yes so if they feel like you're harassing them, they should be upfront and honest if they've changed their minds.

What If They Don't Say Anything at All

Investors get hundreds of emails a day. After all, they give money away for a living. You'd be that popular too if you had that job. Trust me, it's not because of our charming personalities. Sometimes, they miss an email or two.

You're not being too pushy if you send them multiple emails to ensure they've actually seen your deck. This is also another reason to use a tool like Docsend, so you know whether your pitch deck link has been clicked.

Figuring out what someone's personal cell number is and calling or texting them directly if they didn't explicitly give it to you, however, is too pushy. Investors have preferred ways of being contacted and I think you need to respect that. It's fine to leave polite comments on their public social profiles (i.e., "Great post . . . Totally agree with you about having big ambitions from day one. That's why I'd love your feedback on our deck. It's in your email and we're by far the most ambitious plan in your inbox.")

That doesn't mean you should continue you escalate the issue on that same thread.

"Hey, why aren't you responding to me?"
"You have some nerve ignoring me! I know you saw this."

That's just unhinged.

If you really want to do multiple pings, just keep *politely* trying different channels—an email reply to a newsletter post. A LinkedIn comment. A polite reply to the last thing you sent them saying why their feedback in particular was important to you. Why them?

On the other hand, if you're in the middle of the process and they're "ghosting" you (Figure 10.1), you can consider the investor no

Figure 10.1 These are ghosts, drawn by my four-year-old daughter who asked me why my book had no pictures. I told her if she drew me a black-and-white picture, I'd find a way to work it in. These ghost investors are ghosting you because they're busy flying a kite and playing with their ghost friends.

longer interested. A polite closing email thanking them for their time and an indication that you're going to focus on other investors will suffice. Feel free to update them on future progress but lower their chance of closing in your sales funnel to zero.

What to Do If It's a No

When things don't work out with a firm, it's important to realize that every founder gets rejected. Most successful ones get rejected a lot.

The difference is how they respond to it.

Don't get me wrong—a no feels personal. You pitched your heart out, sacrificed a ton to get to this point, and told the story of why your company deserves to exist. The person across the table didn't believe it.

How else could you take it?

But here's the truth: rejection in venture capital is not a verdict on your worth. You might totally be the kind of person this investor would be happy to have work for one of these companies, or even back for another idea.

It's not even necessarily a verdict on your company. Most of the time, it's feedback. It's data. If you can train yourself to hear no that way, rejection becomes one of your most useful tools for getting better.

What a No Really Means

Every rejection contains a reason—even if the investor doesn't say it out loud. Sometimes it's about you: Do they believe you can pull this off? Other times it's about the market: Is this opportunity big enough to matter in their fund? Sometimes it's about timing: is this the moment to back this kind of company?

Too often, founders lump all rejections together as "they didn't get it." That's lazy. Smart founders break down the subtext. They ask:

- Did they doubt my ability to execute?
- Did they question the size of the market?
- Did they dismiss the urgency of the problem?

Or did they actually think I could succeed, but that the outcome would never be big enough for them?

These are four very different no's. They each demand a different response.

Rejection as Market Research

Think about it this way: If a customer says no to your product, you'd never storm out of the room and swear them off forever. You'd want to know why. You'd study their reaction, look for patterns, and adjust.

Fundraising is no different. Every investor who passes is giving you a free data point about how your story is landing. One pass doesn't tell you much. When you start hearing the same questions over and over—"What's your distribution plan?" "How defensible is this?"—that's the market talking back to you.

You can ignore it and keep repeating the same story, or you can sharpen your pitch. Sometimes the insight even pushes you to rethink your strategy itself. Plenty of founders discover their weak spots not in customer meetings, but in investor rejections.

Don't Argue, Don't Vanish

Here's where many founders blow it: they treat rejection like a fight, or like a breakup. They argue with the investor, try to win them over in the room, and leave behind a sour taste. Or they go to the other extreme—they vanish. They treat no as the end of the relationship.

Both are mistakes. No does not mean "never." It usually means "not yet."

Not yet, however, also doesn't mean, "after seeing more of exactly the same thing."

Usually, something has to change. Your initial sales traction with one salesperson needs to be replicated to multiple reps. Your contract size needs to go up.

What matters is what happens after the no. Investors don't want to be cornered or convinced in a single conversation. They want to see what you do with time. Do you keep executing? Do you hit milestones? Do you follow up, not with excuses, but with evidence of progress?

It's important to see the kind of progress that directly addresses the concerns.

I once passed on a company that was getting traction, but only with small customers. I told them that I didn't think they'd be able to sell into the enterprise. They came back to me with an enthusiastic note about all the growth they've been having—all from small customers.

Nice, but I still have the same exact concern that I had before.

Listening, digesting, and being able to directly address someone's issue is what builds trust.

Investors aren't just betting on your idea—they're betting on your ability to absorb feedback, course-correct, and keep moving. If your response to rejection is to sulk or lash out, you've already failed that test.

The Long Game

This isn't *Shark Tank*.

You don't get one shot in front of the cameras and then it's over. Real fundraising is a long game. Investors track founders over years. They watch how you handle setbacks. They remember if you followed up after that early meeting, or if you disappeared until your next raise.

I can't tell you how many times I've seen founders get passed on at the seed stage or even the Series A, only to come back to VCs for a later round when they'd clearly figured it out. In those cases, what changed wasn't the market or even the product—it was the founder.

They kept everyone in the loop. They sent updates. They proved they could execute by de-risking the specific concerns an investor had.

Contrast that with the founders who treat no as a door slammed shut. They never follow up. They resurface two years later, desperate and frustrated, and I have to relearn who they are. That doesn't build confidence.

The same thing often happens with a founder's own investors when they need a bridge or support to put together a next round. If investors haven't heard from you, even if they're your own, you will have failed to built up enough trust for them to continue to support you.

What If the Raise Actually Fails?

Most founders don't plan for what happens if the round just doesn't come together. You set a target, line up the meetings, push hard for weeks or months—and sometimes you still wind up at zero. That doesn't mean you're finished as a founder, and it doesn't even mean this idea is dead. What it means is that you need to pause, reset, and treat the failed raise itself as data.

Too many founders double down on the same pitch to the same people, thinking one more meeting will magically flip a no into a yes. That's rarely how it works—so choosing a point at which it has failed, maybe after a certain amount of outreach and before you're totally out of money and options, is critical.

If you fail when there's literally no money in the bank, then you're dead—so try to fail when you've still got enough resources to try something different.

A failed process is feedback at the process level, not just the individual pitch level. It usually means your story isn't sharp enough, your milestones aren't convincing enough, or the market timing isn't right. Step back and ask: Did I sequence my outreach correctly? Did I try to raise before I had the proof points investors needed? Was my target list even right for the kind of company I'm building?

The second step is triage. If you have runway left, use it to de-risk the next attempt—focus on customer traction, product validation, or revenue that addresses the objections you kept hearing. If you don't have runway, the right move may be to slow down, cut burn, and extend your timeline. Sometimes the smartest play is to not raise for a while, but to go build the proof that will make the next raise work.

Finally, don't disappear. The founders who treat a failed raise as the end of the road vanish from investor inboxes, and those investors assume the worst. The better move is to keep the investors you met in the loop. Send them updates showing that you're still building, still learning, still finding a way forward. The no you got wasn't forever—it was not yet. If you turn that yet into progress, you'll be surprised how many people come back around.

Flipping the Script

Rejection hurts. It always will. But the founders who learn to reframe it—to treat no as part of the process, not the end of it—are the ones who last. They understand that a no is an invitation: to clarify, to adjust, to show progress, to keep building.

And here's the irony: the way you handle rejection is often the very thing that turns it into a future yes.

So don't argue. Don't vanish. Don't take it personally. Instead, collect the data, keep the relationship alive, and make it impossible for the investor not to notice when you come back stronger.

That's how rejection stops being the end of the story—and starts being the beginning of the next chapter.

Final Thoughts

Everyone wants to be a great founder.

You spend a lot of time telling people you're a great founder—first yourself, then people you raise money from, and then people who come to work for you, sacrificing stability at other jobs.

It becomes part of your identity to be great at this, or at least someone whose idea is great.

That's why the ups and downs of the job can be so stressful—winning customers, losing deals, seeing some experiments succeed while others crash and burn.

A founder once asked me why I seemed so stress-free. First of all, everyone stresses, so that's not true. I do, however, keep the impact of the stress at bay with this secret:

I concede that the possibility exists that I might not be good at this—and that's okay.

Also, just because things don't work out in the end, doesn't actually mean you weren't good at it. The truth is probably that you were good at some things, not as good at others, hopefully learning, maybe not learning the right things fast enough—and much of your outcome was probably beyond your control.

For me, oddly enough, the idea of failure keeps me calm and levelheaded. I always like to think it through. When I started a company—something I actually wasn't very good at—early on I had decided that I was willing to sacrifice a lot, but I would never sell my Mustang convertible. Having a clear sense of what would happen if things didn't work out meant there was less uncertainty to be afraid of.

Most of all, I knew I was employable and that I was building out my network the whole time I was starting a company.

If you don't admit that failure is a possibility, your brain can't process even the hint of it. When things don't go right, it goes against how you thought things were "supposed to" go, and against your definition of yourself as someone who always succeeds.

Stress comes from your inability to accept. You can combat that by telling yourself, "Despite the fact that I work hard and follow disciplined thinking, I may not have what it takes to create success here with this idea, at this time—and that's okay."

If you can't handle that reality, you wind up with haywire emotions, misplaced blame, and an inability to observe reality as it is—creating bad feedback loops.

When failure isn't an option, you start doing irrational, sometimes dangerous things for yourself, your team, and your company. Failure is always an option. Some things just won't work out, and you'll need to figure out another plan.

For now, though—you're not there. You know that because you can be honest about its existence and identify what it looks like. That honesty gives you the confidence and focus to keep at it when you're not there yet, and to improve enough to avoid it.

I can fail.

I might not be good.

I am trying really hard every day to be better and to succeed.

All of these things can be true—and healthy—for a founder to tell themselves.

The founders that last the longest aren't the ones who measure themselves by a single outcome. They're curious, not delusional. They know they're not guaranteed or destined for greatness—they're out there earning it.

They experiment, get feedback, accept when they have to change course, and improve without the panic of having to be perfect right now.

Acknowledgments

I'd like to thank my editor, Phil Marino, for not following through on his startup idea after seeing me speak on a panel years ago.

Sure, he could have been the next Steve Jobs, but I'm glad he decided that he'd rather be a business book editor who cold emails opinionated career VCs who make themselves findable through online thought leadership.

I'd also like to thank Fred Wilson, who first suggested that I join Union Square Ventures for my first job at a venture capital firm when I asked him what junior VCs even do.

It was an important lesson that it never hurts to ask.

Also, thanks to Josh Kopelman for taking an unplanned shot on me to help First Round Capital open their New York City office when NYC started really taking off as a startup hub. I had no usable skills and was $34,000 in the hole in credit card debt after failing miserably at my startup—making me perfect for a job that involves taking big risks without actually doing the kind of hard work that founders do.

About the Author

Charlie O'Donnell is a highly sought-after fundraising expert, coach to top VCs and a faculty member teaching entrepreneurship at NYU's Courant Institute. He is the founder of nextNYC, the most active tech community and events platform in New York City.

For over two decades, Charlie has been a mainstay in the NYC startup ecosystem. He began his career as the first analyst at Union Square Ventures after working in General Motors's venture capital and private equity group. In 2009, he helped First Round Capital open its New York office, sourcing early investments in companies such as GroupMe (sold to Skype), Singleplatform (sold to Constant Contact), Moat (sold to Oracle), and Backupify (sold to Datto).

In 2012, he launched Brooklyn Bridge Ventures—backing more than 100 local startups including Hungryroot, Brigit (sold to Upbound Group), Shortcut, Radformation, and Imagen. Known as the most accessible early-stage investor in New York, Charlie prioritized inclusivity: 40% of BBV's portfolio companies were female-founded, 30% had a BIPOC founder, and 9% had a Black founder.

Charlie was named to *Business Insider*'s 100 Most Influential People in NY Tech five times and featured on *City & State*'s Tech Power 50.

Outside of tech, Charlie co-founded the Brooklyn Bridge Park Boathouse, which welcomes thousands of paddlers to the East River with the help of hundreds of local volunteers.

Charlie is a member of the Brooklyn Triathlon Club, a softball player, and ice hockey goalie. He lives in Park Slope, Brooklyn, with his wife and daughter. His co-op board president suffering is matched only by his lifelong fandom of the New York Mets.

Since 2004, his writing has lived at www.thisisgoingtobebig.com, which you can access by scanning this QR code:

Index

A
AI. *See* artificial intelligence
Amin, Kareem, 10
angel groups, 23, 145
angel investors, 44, 96, 144–145, 167, 218
artificial intelligence (AI), 1, 45, 64, 180

B
bad-fit investors, 159
bad ideas, overcommitment to, 88–90
banks, raising funds from, 142
beggars (founder persona), 15
Best, Candis, 41
Bezos, Jeff, 141
bias of investors, xv–xvi, 33–34, 103, 122, 201
blank-check teams, 60, 183–184
board, 69–70
    meeting, 70
    pre-board, members, 70–72

boardroom chaos in venture capital firms, 48
Braze, 208–209
brokers, 91, 93
budget, 119
    finding employees within, 65–66
    marketing, 105
    operational, 122
    strategic, 122
Burks Solomon, Jewel, 38
Burnham, Brad, 44
business modeler (pre-board persona), 70–71

C
Cap tables, 109–110
Carse, James, xvi
cautious founders, 128–129
celebrity founders, 13
Cerilli, Wiley, 107–108
Climate Tech VC (newsletter), 59–60

co-founders, 26, 32, 61–65, 134, 137
Cohen, Emily, 208
cold pitches, 92
Collab Capital, 38
community trust, 113–114
compensation for team members, 68–69
competition, 6, 85–87
compounding growth, 5, 130, 168
computer science, women in, 31
confidence, 19–20, 77, 102, 121, 129, 130, 160, 167, 168, 203
connections with investors, building, 172–173
convertible notes, 181, 217
conviction, 111, 131, 195, 203
credentialed academics (founder persona), 12
credibility, 10, 12, 15, 53, 118, 144, 195
crowdfunding, 142–143
crowd investing, 143
curiosity, 52–53, 190, 195
curiosity > thought leadership flywheel, 54–55
customer(s), 84, 85, 112, 205, 206
acquisition of, 6
conversion of networks into, 75–77
feedback from, 88, 106
pain, 13, 187
red flags, 109
and traction, 188–189

D

decision paralysis in venture capital firms, 47
demos, 204–205
dilution, 7, 124, 125
distressed investing, 109
Docsend, 219
Dorsey, Jack, 8, 184, 211
drivers (mindset)
resourced, 17, 18–21
underresourced, 17, 21–22
Dunbar, Robin, 56

E

early-stage investing, 109, 115–116, 117
e-commerce, 9, 151
emails
Heartbeat Emails, 57–60
initial, 182–183, 189
employees, 61
right mix, finding, 65–66
talking to potential employees, 133

entrepreneurial mindset, 18
equity, 67, 69, 98, 110
equity round, 127, 181, 216
excuses of founders, 104–105
execution
   and belief, 129–130
   hesitation of cautious founders, 128–129
   impact of hesitation, 130
   and non-VCs, 143–144
   trust, 113, 128
executives (founder persona), 11–12
expectations of yourself, 104, 106

F
Facebook, 142, 149, 150–151
failed raise, 224–225
family
   raising funds from, 140–142, 179–180
   support of, 76–79
family offices, 11, 145–146, 153
fast founders, 127–128, 131
fast risk, 130–131
fear
   of being wasteful, 129
   FOMO (fear of missing out), 145, 155–158
   of investors, 112–113
feedback, xvii, 69, 78–79
   asking the right questions, 82–84
   best kind of, 79–82
   from customers, 88, 106
   failed process, 225
   from peers, 175, 177
Feld, Brad, 52
Field, Dylan, 185
Figma, 185
financial models, 131–138
finite games, xvi–xvii
First Round Capital, xviii, 8, 9, 44
FOMO (fear of missing out), 145, 155–158
founders of color, 33, 34
founder time, cost of, 99
friends
   raising funds from, 140–142, 179–180
   support of, 76–79
fundability scorecard, 24–27
fundraising cushion, 123
fundraising pipeline, 153–154

G
gamblers, 139–140
General Catalyst, xiv
ghost investors, 219, 220–221
"gone rogue" investor, 215–216
Google, 150
great teams, 184–185

H

hacker-pivoters (founder persona), 10, 15
Hamed, Ali, 116
Hargreaves, Brad, 60
Hayes, Rob, 102
Heartbeat Emails, 57–60
    effectiveness of, 57
    payoff of, 59–60
    recipients of, 57–58
    structure of, 58
    style of, 58–59
hesitation
    of cautious founders, 128–129
    impact of, 130
high-net-worth individuals, 143–144
hiring checklist, 69
hustling emerging managers (venture capitalist), 44–45
hybrid funding model, 38
hypothesis testing, 69, 82–83

I

Iger, Bob, 3
ikigai, 53–55
industry icons (venture capitalist), 45–46
industry insiders (founder persona), 10–11
infinite games, xvii
influencer founders, 13
insider (pre-board persona), 71
interested investors, 211–212
    commitment to invest, 216–219
    "gone rogue" investor, 215–216
    lack of response from, 219–221
    and leading, 213, 214–215
    turning into committed investors, 212–213
interviews
    curiosity > thought leadership flywheel, 54–55
    with investors, 173–174
    with successful founders/leaders, 174–175
introduction to investors, 79, 80, 91, 175
investor leads, qualifying, 175
investor qualification process, 176

J

junior folks (venture capitalist), 43–44
junior staffers (founder persona), 11

K

Kardashian, Kim, 13
Kawasaki, Guy, 52
Kopelman, Josh, 9

L

lead, fundraising, 216–217
leading process, 213, 214–215
learning, 83, 86, 117
Lederman, Drew, 208
level setting, 24, 107–108
lifeline (pre-board persona), 71–72
LinkedIn, 9, 42, 193
Lore, Marc, 184

M

Magnuson, Bill, 208–209
marketing, 82, 88–89, 130
marketing budget, 105
market(s), 5, 151, 196, 207
    economics, 187
    knowledge, 112
    product-market fit, 120, 136, 137, 208
    right, 185–187
    scaling ability, 187
    size, 5, 151
    structure, 186–187
    tailwinds, 186
    validation, 78
meetings, 70, 72–74
milestones, 119, 120–121, 135, 218
mindset, 15–16
    resourced, 16–21, 22–23
    underresourced, 16–18, 21–22, 23–24
misaligned incentives in venture capital firms, 47–48
missionary founders, 12–13, 15
Moran, Na'ama, 2

N

networks, 11, 16, 39–42, 120
    and brokers, 91
    connecting with investors, 172–173
    conversion into customers, 75–77
    creating, 92–93
    and founder excitement, 77
    founders with venture-backed friends, 39–40
    friends and family support, 76–79
    Heartbeat Emails, 57–60
    and *ikigai*, 54–55
    maintaining, 51, 56
    peer groups, 175–177
    of resourced drivers, 20
    of resourced passengers, 23
    role of curiosity in building, 52–53
    of success, uneven distribution of, 40–41
    testing, 115
newsletters, 59–60, 84
no-lead round, 215
novel ideas, 190–191

O

Oculus, 142, 149, 150–151
Odeo, 8, 211
old guys (venture capitalist), 46
OpenAI, 164–165
operational budgeting, 122
operational trust, 112
optionality, 129, 215–216
outsiders (founder persona), 14, 15
ownership, 123–125
    and profitability, 126
    secret for owning more, 125–127

P

partner churn in venture capital firms, 47
passengers (mindset)
    resourced, 17, 22–23
    underresourced, 17, 23–24
peer groups, 175–177
pitch(es), 101–102, 152–155, 203–205
    advice, 96
    aggressiveness of ambition in, 167–169
    ask of founders, 121–123
    and bias of investors, 103
    cold, 92
    conversation, control of, 206–207
    convincing investors in, 102–103
    deck, 115, 153, 155, 182, 189–190, 197–200, 201–202, 203, 219
    flow, controlling, 202
    gender differences in, 33
    level of detail in forecasting, 169–170
    narration in, 202–203
    pattern-matching, 209
    planting ideas, 190–192
    sandbagging, 165–167
    scrutiny of, 159, 161–162
    talking about problems, 192–194
    and VC partner meetings, 196–200
    vision with growth potential, 162–165
    winning the attention of investors, 201
Planeteer Capital, 59
plausibility, 112–113, 132, 208
PMF. *See* product-market fit
podcasts, 52, 94, 173–174
possibility, pitching, 162–165
power law distribution of VC fund, 149
pre-board, 73
    business modeler, 70–71

insider, 71
lifeline, 71–72
pre-seed round, 74, 156, 178, 180–181
presentation deck, 202
product-market fit (PMF), 120, 136, 137, 208
professional angels, 144–145
profitability, and ownership, 126
Pro + Rookie model, 67–68
prototypes, 27, 149, 151
Purdom, Sophie, 59–60

R
Rabois, Keith, 45
read deck, 153, 202
red flags, investment, 109–110
rejection, 221–224
   follow up after, 223–224
   as market research, 222
   reasons for, 221–222
   responding to, 222–223, 225
repeat founders, 26, 184
rescue round, 178
resourced mindset, 16–18
   drivers, 17, 18–21
   passengers, 17, 22–23
revenue, 27, 96
risk
   fast, 130–131

and resourced drivers, 19
slow, 130–131
tolerance, 38, 63, 139–147
rounds, funding, 177–179
friends-and-family round, 179–180
no-lead round, 215
pre-seed, 74, 156, 178, 180–181
seed, 127, 178, 181
Series A, 178, 181

S
SAFE (Simple Agreement for Future Equity), 26, 70, 181, 216, 217
sales skills, 102
sandbagging, 165–167
scrutiny, 7, 74, 159, 161–162
sector with wreckage, 27
seed round, 127, 178, 181
seedstrapping, 126
Series A round, 178, 181
Shapiro, Julian, 190
Shopify, 212
skepticism, being comfortable with, 102–103
slow risk, 130–131
SLP. *See* Startup Leadership Program
social capital, 79, 80, 179
social media, 42, 84, 88

social proof, 98, 118, 217
SPACE agreement, 38
specificity, 26, 177, 212
speed, 6, 26–27, 130
Square, 8
stage-based financial model, 135–138
   build and test, 135–136
   effectiveness of, 137–138
   founder-driven sales/ limited go to market, 136
   post PMF, 136–137
startup advice
   and assumptions, 98
   cost of, 98
   direct participation of advisors, 96–98
startup communities, curation of, 175
Startup Leadership Program (SLP), 41
Stebbings, Harry, 52, 173
strategic budgeting, 122

T

TAM slide, 204
team, startup, 49, 60–67, 182
   avoiding pre-rejection, 67
   bio of, 195–196
   blank-check teams, 60, 183–184
   co-founders, 26, 32, 61–65, 134, 137
   compensation guardrails, 68–69
   drama, 109
   and equity, 67
   "everyone else" category, 185
   finding employees, 65–66
   great team, 184–185
   hiring checklist, 69
   and ideas, 49–51
   pressure testing of, 66
   Pro + Rookie model, 67–68
   relationship building, 66–67
technical co-founders, 26, 32
technical talent, 31–32, 104–105
tech sector
   and venture capital funding, 30, 31
   women in, 31–32
testimonials, 206
therapy, 160–161
Thesis Driven (newsletter), 60
three-week investor decision timeline, 156
time horizon, 139–147

traction, 88, 107, 188–189, 196, 204, 207
transparency, 117
triage, after failed raise, 225
trust, 111–114, 223, 224
   building, xvii, 51
   community, 113–114
   and early-stage investing, 115–116, 117–118
   execution, 113, 128
   operational, 112
Twenty Minute VC, The (podcast), 52, 173–174

U

underrepresented founders, 91–92, 170
underresourced mindset, 16–18
   drivers, 17, 21–22
   passengers, 17, 23–24
unequal partnerships, in venture capital firms, 46–47
Union Square Ventures, xviii, 44, 84
unit economics, 5, 132

V

validation, 77–78, 80, 83, 113–114
VCs. *See* venture capitalists

venture-backed friends, founders with, 39–40
venture capital, 4, 8, 158. *See also* pitch(es)
   bias in, 33–34
   checklist for taking, 5–7
   as a financial product, 37–38
   funding to women, xiv, 29–30, 31–33, 206
   math, 148–151
   and technical talent pool, 31–32
venture capital firms, dysfunctional
   boardroom chaos, 48
   decision paralysis, 47
   misaligned incentives, 47–48
   partner churn, 47
   unequal partnerships, 46–47
venture capitalists (VCs), 121, 145, 147–148, 175
   hustling emerging managers, 44–45
   industry icons, 45–46
   junior folks, 43–44
   old guys, 46
   partner meetings, 196–200
venture vultures, 94–95
viral adoption, 27

W
wealthy hobbyists (founder persona), 14
Weiner, Jeff, 185
Williams, Ev, 8
Wilson, Fred, 44, 84
women
  as big risk takers, 170
  in computer science, 31
  pitches by, 33
  in tech industry, 31, 32
  venture capital funding to, xiv, 29–30, 31–33, 206

X
X-for-Y comparisons, 204, 209

Z
Zuzunaga, Andrés, 54